"The life I now live⟨ ⟩
faith in the Son of God [Jesus],
who loved me and gave himself for me."

GALATIANS 2:20

Being gospel fluent inevitably shapes
how we live, which then affects how
we engage with the world around us.
The good news is good news again;
and where the beautiful reminder
of what God did for us in Christ can
break through the chaos and usher
us into the love of God; where the
gospel isn't an appendix to a sermon
but the mountain on which all
preaching stands; and where we can
recognize that the gospel doesn't
just save us but keeps us.

JACKIE HILL PERRY

Praise for *Gospel Fluency*

"I have known Jeff for over a decade now, and his heart beats for the church to be all that God has called her to be in Christ. He is not just an ideas man – he is on the ground living out the truths you read in this book. As the culture shifts and attractional ministry fades, Jeff will be a faithful guide for us all."

MATT CHANDLER

Lead Pastor, The Village Church, Dallas, TX; President, Acts 29 Church Planting Network

"It's easy to forget how good the good news of the gospel is. This practical book will help you to see that good news, and to share it with others."

RUSSELL MOORE

President, Southern Baptist Ethics & Religious Liberty Commission

"I've been wanting to have a resource from Jeff on this topic for a very long time. It is so, so, so needed. As I've worked with different Christians from several churches around the city of Chicago, I've witnessed the lack of gospel understanding that has permeated many 'solid' churches. I will personally hand out copies of this book like gospel tracts."

JACKIE HILL PERRY

Poet, writer, and hip-hop artist

"Jeff has written a book that will be around a long time by reforming evangelism in a fresh way."

BOB ROBERTS

Senior Pastor, Northwood Church; author, *Bold as Love* and *Lessons from the East*

"We need books like Gospel Fluency to both ground us in our practice of the gospel and raise us out of living our daily life in the cultural drift."

DANIEL MONTGOMERY

Lead Pastor, Sojourn Community Church, Louisville, KY; Founder of the Sojourn Network; author of *Faithmapping* and *Leadership Mosaic*

"Jeff calls us back to the gospel, not as a trite word to throw around in Christian circles but as a life-changing language in which we grow more fluent as we use it in community. The analogy to learning a foreign language helps us envision how to become fluent in the gospel, working, eating, even dreaming immersed in the good news of Jesus and how that changes everything. This is an extremely practical and helpful book!"

WENDY ALSUP

Teacher, blogger, and author of *Is the Bible Good for Women?* and *Practical Theology for Women*

GOSPEL FLUENCY
HANDBOOK

A PRACTICAL GUIDE TO
SPEAKING THE TRUTHS OF JESUS
INTO THE EVERYDAY STUFF OF LIFE

JEFF VANDERSTELT
& BEN CONNELLY

SATURATE   PUBLISHING

EVERY CHURCH. EVERY PERSON.
EVERY PLACE.

Gospel Fluency Handbook

Copyright © 2017 by Jeff Vanderstelt and Ben Connelly

Published by **Saturate**

227 Bellevue Way NE, #224
Bellevue, WA 98004
www.saturatetheworld.com

ISBN: 978-1-7324913-2-8

eBook ISBN: 978-0-9968493-3-3

Cover and book design I Charlie Apel

Editing I Lisa Kukkamaa Baker

Printed in USA

Third Printing 2018

Contents

ENHANCE YOUR *GOSPEL FLUENCY
HANDBOOK* EXPERIENCE WITH THE

Companion Videos!

Watch the accompanying video each week as you walk through the *Handbook* with your community. Learning and immersing ourselves in the gospel is hard work! We need all the help we can get! In this nine-part video series, Jeff Vanderstelt provides a great launching point into discussion each week, helping groups grasp the concepts and dive into the practice of becoming gospel fluent.

VIDEOS TO ENHANCE YOUR WEEKLY LEARNING:

INTRO   *What is Gospel Fluency and Why is it Important?*

WEEK 1   *Everyone is an Unbeliever*

WEEK 2   *The Gospel Story*

WEEK 3   *The Gospel in Me, Part 1*

WEEK 4   *The Gospel in Me, Part 2*

WEEK 5   *The Gospel with Us, Part 1*

WEEK 6   *The Gospel with Us, Part 2*

WEEK 7   *The Gospel to Others, Part 1*

WEEK 8   *The Gospel to Others, Part 2*

EXTRAS:

Leader's Video

Vision for this Handbook

Sharing Communion in Community

A Note of Thanks

We are honored that you picked up this Saturate resource. Our prayer is that God will use the inadequate words in the following pages to help you grow in his completely sufficient Word, and that over the coming weeks the gospel will begin to flow out of you more naturally, into the varied situations, conversations, and relationships of your everyday life.

The introduction will serve as a guide for you as you begin this eight-week journey, especially if it's a journey you're taking with others (which for many reasons, both theological and practical, we hope it is). As you jump in beyond that, we encourage you to think creatively about some of the suggestions we make and practices we encourage. If one doesn't specifically fit your group, don't feel locked into any one way; instead, prayerfully consider and discuss different ways to put principles into practice.

Enjoy the coming weeks of growing together, and may the gospel be increasingly in your heart and mind as you join many across the world in becoming increasingly fluent in applying the good news of Jesus in your life, for his glory and your joy, forever.

JEFF VANDERSTELT
& BEN CONNELLY

Introduction

"I'm an unbeliever. So are you," Jeff Vanderstelt tells us in his book, *Gospel Fluency*. "I struggle with unbelief on a daily basis," he continues. "I have a conversation with my wife, and when she points out something I've yet to get better at, I hear the word *failure* in my head. I try to lead a good conversation about the Bible at the dinner table with my children, but instead of eager beavers on the edges of their seats, I get slouched bodies and rolling eyes. *Bad father.* I teach on being a good neighbor, one who knows the stories of the people who live on your street, but since I moved into my current neighborhood, I know only the story of failed attempts to meet people. *Hypocrite.* Unbelief.

"I slip in and out of believing God's word about me and trusting in his work for me. Jesus gave his life to make me a new creation. He died to forgive me of my sins and change my identity from *sinner* to *saint*, from *failure* to *faithful*, and from *bad* to *good* and even *righteous* and *holy*. But I forget what he has said about me. I forget what he has done for me. And sometimes it isn't forgetfulness. Sometimes it's just plain unbelief. I know these things. I just don't believe them.

"I am an unbeliever. Not every moment, of course. But I have those moments. So do you. I'm certain of it."

You may have picked up this *Gospel Fluency Handbook* because you've realized that there are areas of your life—your normal, everyday, busy life—where you disbelieve God and his goodness and his gospel, and you're hoping to pursue a deeper belief. Maybe you've been keenly aware of this disbelief for a long time, even weighted down by guilt and shame over it, and are hoping for a way out. Maybe you're new to the reality of Jesus and his gospel—or at least that it actually matters to your everyday life. Or maybe you're simply looking into this "gospel" as someone who stands in firm unbelief of it. Whoever you are, and whatever your motive for picking up this resource, simply because you're a human you're an unbeliever!

HOW TO USE THIS HANDBOOK

The first goal of the *Gospel Fluency Handbook* is to help you become fluent in the gospel—in other words, to help you move from unbelief to belief, in whatever area(s) of your life you find it difficult to believe God's promises, and live according to that belief. The second goal, which we hope naturally flows from the first, is to help you speak the truths of Jesus into the everyday stuff of life as we together become a more gospel-fluent people. To that end, we've crafted this resource as an interactive guide to walk you step-by-step into immersing your mind, heart, soul, and life in the gospel. It's not a book; books are generally designed to give information, and to be read cover to cover, often in just a few days. While the content here accompanies a book—Jeff Vanderstelt's *Gospel Fluency: Speaking the Truths of Jesus into the Everyday Stuff of Life* (Crossway, 2017)—this *Handbook* can also be an independent resource[1]. Each week of the *Handbook* follows a simple format: three sets of personal Readings and Reflections, about the same length as this introduction, then a weekly guide for Group Discussion and Exercises.

1. **Readings and Reflections**: The majority of each week is comprised of three Readings, which are excerpts from *Gospel Fluency* and related scriptures, upon which to read and reflect. Each Reading is followed by a personal Reflection with questions to prayerfully answer, thoughts to respond to, and ways to help you practice the content of that Reading. Each set of Readings and Reflections should take no more than 30-45 minutes to complete. After the third Reading and Reflection of each week, there's a blank page titled "Look Back," simply for you to reflect on what you've learned over that week.

---

[1]. Content from *Gospel Fluency* is summarized in each week's Readings, and for participants who want to go deeper, each week indicates corresponding chapters in *Gospel Fluency*, if you choose to read that.

2. **Group Discussion and Exercises**: A theme throughout both *Gospel Fluency* and this *Handbook* is our need for others. After completing the three Readings and Reflections each week, the week closes with a guide for how groups can discuss, help each other, and practice that week's concepts together. We recommend your group meets weekly, and that each week includes a meal. Each week's discussion and exercises will take at least an hour: plan well, to give yourself ample time to walk through them well. One suggestion is to focus your time together on the exercises, rather than trying to address everything given in each week's Group Discussion: pick a couple questions from those given each week, and move through them quickly enough to give yourselves plenty of time for that week's Group Exercise.

3. **Supplemental Videos**: A video series has been created as supplemental and additional material for each week of the *Handbook*. Please go to **www.saturatetheworld.com/gf** and click on "video series". Enter this download code **gfhv20** for 20% off the videos.

Here's one final note regarding the coming weeks, as we acknowledge the reality of our busy lives: the Handbook works best if you try to diligently carry out each week's Readings and Reflections. Of course, you may miss a Reading and Reflection here or there, but if you just breeze through, you've missed the benefit of its design, and you've wasted your time and money. We'll strongly encourage you to set aside the time—on average, one Reading and Reflection per every two days of the coming eight weeks—and devote yourself to this process for this short season.

As an alternate, slower schedule, each of the *Handbook*'s "Weeks" can be divided into two calendar weeks: complete Reading and Reflection 1 and 2, then meet and walk through the related Group Discussion and Exercises the first week; the second week complete Reading and Reflection 3 and "Look Back" then meet and walk through the related Group Discussion and Exercises. This schedule will take you longer, but if it helps everyone participate fully, it may be worth it.

STARTING POINT EXERCISES

Before we get to the first Reading and Reflection, and first Group Discussion Guide included in this introduction, we want to give you two exercises to complete, which would set you on the best possible footing as we begin this journey together—especially if you're taking that journey with a community. Both revolve around the concept of "story," and you'll come back to both later in the *Handbook*.

1. **Share your own stories.** The best "first step" to take, whether you've known those you're walking with for awhile or whether you're a newly formed group, is to know each other's stories. Knowing each person will set you up well, will add a level of comfort, and will give each other a sense of "permission" to speak honestly with each other over the coming weeks. There are many ways to tell your story, but at this point in this *Handbook*, we'll point you to two methods. Choose one and walk through it, preparing to share your story at your First Meeting.

   O **Method One: "Instagram Stories":** Each box on pages 14–15 represents a different part of your story. For each part of the story, draw a still-frame picture that captures the essence of that stage. Prepare to talk to your community through your story using the pictures at your first meeting. At this point, the only stipulation is that you be honest—even let yourself be stretched in vulnerability! It doesn't matter how good your drawings are; this is simply a way for you to tell your story and to share it with others.

   O **Method Two: "Pillars":** Reflect on three key events in your life which have shaped, influenced, and directed the other elements of your life. Using the images on pages 8–9, write about the event, the situations or people surrounding it, etc., and why/how it shaped the other elements of your life. At this point, the only stipulation is that you be honest—even let yourself be stretched in vulnerability!

2. **Tell God's story.** As we'll see in the coming weeks, gospel fluency is reliant on knowing the "gospel story"—the themes of the Bible. Before diving into week 1, we encourage you to carve out time and space to walk through God's story together. Two resources might help with this, the "Story Formed Way" or "The True Story" (both available at **saturatetheworld.com/gf**). Whether you use one of these resources or find a different way to walk through the story of the Bible, knowing God's story will be invaluable for your group as you work through the next eight weeks.

    To share each others' Instagram or Pillar stories and God's story, we'll challenge you to find an extended time to meet *before* you dive into Week 1 together. A few helpful suggestions…

    O You might plan one extended meeting after your first one, specifically designed to share your stories and walk through the story of God.

    O You might plan to meet weekly for the same amount of time but prepare to devote a few weeks specifically to each others' stories and the story of God.

    O You might (and this is our #1 suggestion) plan an overnight retreat to get away, spend time together, and give yourselves plenty of time and space—outside the context of everyday life—for stories.

You may think it odd that our first suggestion in this *Handbook* is to press "pause." It is admittedly illogical in some ways! And we're well aware that there's never a convenient moment for giving more time to something like this—especially an overnight retreat! But please see the willingness to request this of you, from the very start, as a sign of the importance we see in sharing your stories and sharing God's story—and in doing so before you dive into the *Handbook*. It truly is that important.

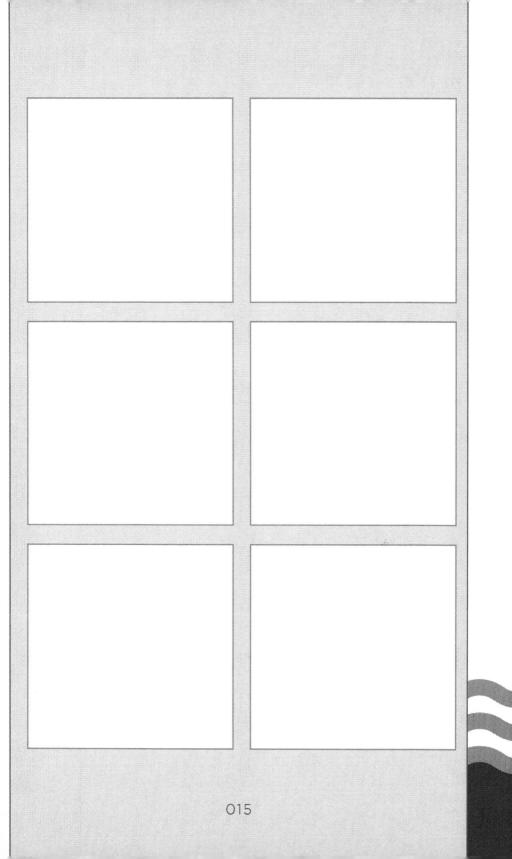

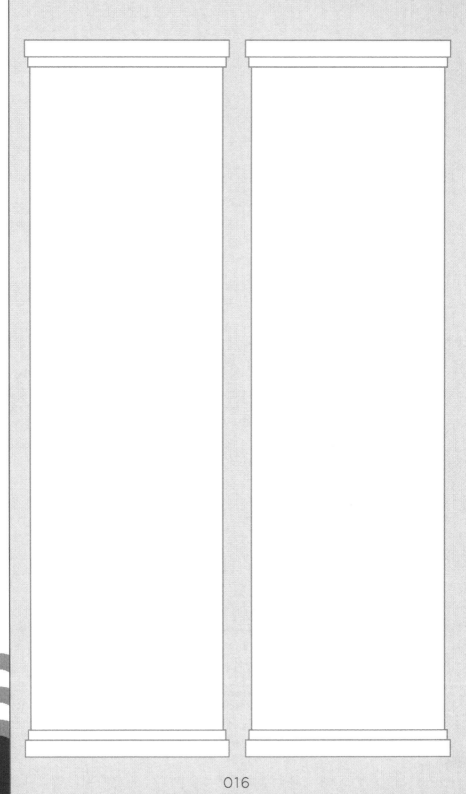

NOTES

THE GOAL OF THIS HANDBOOK

If the majority of this first Reading has been an overview and how to use this resource for a brief season in your life, we close with the overarching hope, which we pray extends far beyond these eight weeks. Here are the closing words of Jeff's first chapter of *Gospel Fluency*: "I wrote this book because I love unbelievers and I know God does too. He loves you and wants to save you from your unbelief.

"I believe the only hope for all of us is the gospel of Jesus Christ and a community that lives life together while proclaiming this gospel into each others' lives daily—a gospel-fluent community. Jesus said we are to make disciples who can make disciples (see Matt. 28:18–20), and a disciple of Jesus should know, believe, and be able to speak the gospel. He or she also should be capable of leading others to know, believe, and speak the gospel.

"My hope is that this book, first of all, will bring about hope and healing for you as you come to believe and apply the truths of the gospel to your life. I also hope that you and others around you will become fluent in the gospel, so that together you will be able to lead others to find hope and help in Jesus in every part of their lives.

"I am more certain than ever that apart from belief in the gospel, sinners will suffer everlasting punishment and saints will fail to live lives that bring glory and honor to Jesus Christ. So it is my hope that more sinners will be saved from condemnation and more saints will be set free to overcome sin, fear, and insecurity in their everyday existence. I hope that this book moves you from unbelief to more belief in the gospel of Jesus Christ and equips you to help others do the same."

Personal Reflections to Complete Before Your First Meeting

1. How would you briefly define the gospel?

2. How would you describe being "fluent" in something? In what areas in your life—whether a language, skill, process, etc.—would you describe yourself as being fluent? How did you become fluent in that/those area(s)?

3. Is your experience more that the gospel applies to all of life, or just certain aspects/portions? Whatever your answer, how do you think that belief has come about?

4. As the Apostle Paul starts to close his first letter to the church at Corinth, he says this: "For I delivered to you as of first importance what I also received: that Christ died for our sins in accordance with the Scriptures, that he was buried, that he was raised on the third day in accordance with the Scriptures, and that he appeared to Cephas, then to the twelve. Then he appeared to more than five hundred brothers at one time, most of whom are still alive, though some have fallen asleep. Then he appeared to James, then to all the apostles. Last of all, as to one untimely born, he appeared also to me. For I am the least of the apostles, unworthy to be called an apostle, because I persecuted the church of God. But by the grace of God I am what I am, and his grace toward me was not in vain. On the contrary, I worked harder than any of them, though it was not I, but the grace of God that is with me. Whether then it was I or they, so we preach and so you believed." (1 Cor. 15:3-11)

- What are the elements of "the gospel" Paul lists here?

- Why does he say that the gospel is "of first importance"?

- From this text and otherwise, what do you know of Paul's life and belief—or unbelief—that would cause him to write that he is "the least of these… unworthy to be called an apostle"?

○ How did the good news of the gospel change Paul's unbelief into belief?

○ In what ways does Paul's example give you hope for your own areas of unbelief? (Belief is, after all, the goal of Paul's final words above!)

5. Slowly read back through the text from 1 Corinthians: As you do, make it your prayer that God would help you remember—and believe and rest in—this truth. Consider writing out your thoughts and prayers as you reflect.

6. Do you have any confusion about how the coming weeks will work? What avenue(s) of pausing to share each others' stories and God's story can you make work?

Group Discussion

Based on this Reading and Reflection, honestly discuss these questions with your faith community. Boldly speak truth in love to, and humbly hear truth in love from, each other. Encourage, exhort, commit to help, celebrate, and even rebuke each other in these areas.

1. Did we all do the Reading and Reflection? Assuming yes, what stood out to you? What was new? What was exciting or hopeful? What was difficult? Is there anything that raised questions or confusion?

2. After the Reflection, what was your view of the gospel—and do you think it's a healthy, biblical view?

3. From the Reflection, what stuck out to you as you considered the concept of "fluency"? What does it mean in relation to the gospel?

The next questions are the most logistical in the entire Handbook; they're important as you begin this journey together, to make sure everyone is on the same page. Consider each question through the lens of "discipleship together"—how would you discuss each, if those around you were an actual, healthy, nuclear family?

4. Do we have a weekly time and place we can all commit to meet for a couple hours, to share a family meal and discuss each week's theme?

We'll meet on:

	day	AM PM	time		place

5. Will we all commit to fully giving ourselves to the weekly rhythm of prep work and group meetings, and can we agree to be honest and open with each other—even when things aren't always easy or comfortable? (If there's anything that makes it hard for anyone to say "yes," work through that as a community, humbly speaking truth in love to each other.)

6. As a community, how can we best serve each other as we work through each week's Readings and Reflections? (For example, do verbal processors need to walk through each day together? What accountability might we need, at least during the first couple weeks, to stay on target?)

7. One recommendation is sharing a meal together during each week's meeting: How will our community carry this out? (For example, will the host provide? Will we all claim a week or two, and rotate through bringing food? Will we do themed potlucks?)

8. Decide how we want to take care of children during our weekly family meals. (For example, do we hire babysitters—if so do we all pitch in for the cost, or just parents? Do we rotate through watching kids? Will they stay with us—for dinner or for the whole meeting?)

9. How do we want to carry out the sharing of stories—God's Story and each others' Instagrams and Pillars? (Make a plan to carve out extended time and space together for this—whether all at once or over a few weeks.)

✳NOTE✳

Enrich your learning and experience for this week by watching the companion video at **saturatetheworld.com/gf**

PRAY

As you wrap up your first meeting together, pray for those in your group, and have someone pray for your coming weeks' journey together.

Gospel Fluency

WEEK 1

This first week lays the foundation for the rest of your journey through the Handbook. Following chapters 1–3 of *Gospel Fluency*, we'll consider the concepts of belief vs. unbelief, speaking the truth in love, and living with God's story as our dominant worldview. While the Readings and Reflections contain some objective and doctrinal elements, we encourage you to jump right in and be honest and personal, since the subjective and experiential elements are equally important parts of this week's groundwork.

Everyone is an Unbeliever

WEEK 1, READING 1

Thoughtfully read the following excerpts, or for more context and a deeper dive, read chapter 1 of *Gospel Fluency*.

I'm an unbeliever. So are you.

"*Wait*," you're thinking. "What are you doing writing a book about the gospel of Jesus Christ if you're an unbeliever? And what do you know about me? Who do you think I am?" I grew up believing that people fall into two categories: you are either a believer or an unbeliever; you either believe in Jesus Christ and what he has done for us or you don't. Now, after more than twenty-five years as a pastor, I see that every one of us is an unbeliever, including me—at least in some areas of our lives.

Don't misunderstand me. I do believe there are some who are

regenerate children of God and others who are not yet. There are those who have been given new life through faith in Jesus. They have become new creations and have been given fresh starts because of their faith in Jesus Christ and what he has done for them. And I believe there are others who are still dead in their sins and not yet truly alive in Christ.

When I say we are all unbelievers, I mean we still have places in our lives where we don't believe God. There are spaces where we don't trust his word and don't believe that what he accomplished in Jesus Christ is enough to deal with our past or what we are facing in this moment or the next. We don't believe his word is true or his work is sufficient. We don't believe. We are unbelievers . . .

It's possible that even though you are familiar with Jesus, you have yet to believe in Jesus for yourself, for your life. Or maybe you have come to faith in Jesus, but it hasn't really changed what you do daily or how you engage in the everyday stuff of life.

The apostle Paul said to the believers in Jesus in Galatia, "The life I now live in the flesh I live by faith in the Son of God [Jesus], who loved me and gave himself for me" (Gal. 2:20). They had started with faith in Jesus, but they were putting their faith and hope in something else to make them right instead of Jesus. Paul called them back to an awareness that the good news about Jesus—the gospel—is for all of life: everything. A life of true living is a life of faith in Jesus, a life of believing in Jesus in the everyday stuff of life. God is intent on making everything about Jesus because it is *through him* that all things came into existence and it is *in him* that they are sustained.

God also wants to rescue you from unbelief and sanctify you to become like Jesus. *Sanctification* is just a big word for becoming more and more *like* Jesus through faith *in* Jesus. You *become like* what you *believe in*. So becoming like Jesus requires believing in Jesus more and more in every part of your life. Sanctification is moving from unbelief in Jesus to belief in Jesus in the everyday stuff of life.

You're not there yet, are you? Neither am I. We're still unbelievers who need Jesus more—in more ways and more places.

We all face daily struggles and battles, sometimes from enemies we can't even see. We hear lies and accusations. We struggle with temptations, and we are often deceived. We hear words that were spoken over us when we were younger, echoing in our hearts in ways that don't breed life to our souls. We look at our present situations and wish they were better. And many of us face uncertain futures that, without God, cause us to lead lives of anxiety, worry, and fear.

We all need help because we can come up with plenty of reasons not to believe, not to hope, not to trust in God's word and work for us. We need the gospel, and we need to become a gospel-fluent people. We need to know how to believe and speak the truths of the gospel—the good news of God—in and into the everyday stuff of life. In other words, we need to know how to address the struggles of life and the everyday activities we engage in with what is true of Jesus: the truths of what he accomplished through his life, death, and resurrection, and, as a result, what is true of us as we put our faith in him. The gospel has the power to affect everything in our lives.

Thoughtfully read the following passages of Scripture related to today's theme. Take a few moments to write down words and phrases that particularly struck you, as well as any thoughts or personal applications they prompted. Make these words a prayer to God.

Matthew 28:18–20

John 1:12–13

2 Corinthians 5:17

Ephesians 1:22–23, 2:1–10

Colossians 1:15–20

Everyone is an Unbeliever

WEEK 1, REFLECTION 1

To apply the concepts of this week's "Reading #1" in your everyday life, pray that God will open your eyes and guide you, then answer the following questions and complete the exercises.

1. Considering the content you read, how would you define unbelief in God?

2. What does unbelief in God produce in the way we think, talk, and act in our everyday lives?

3. As mentioned in your reading, "We all face daily struggles and battles, sometimes from enemies we can't even see. We hear lies and accusations. We struggle with temptations, and we are often deceived. We hear words that were spoken over us when we were younger, echoing in our hearts in ways that don't breed life to our souls. We look at our present situations and wish they were better. And many of us face uncertain futures that, without God, cause us to lead lives of anxiety, worry, and fear. We all need help because we can come up with plenty of reasons not to believe, not to hope, not to trust in God's word and work for us."

Over the course of this *Handbook*, your personal readings and reflections and your group discussions and exercises will help you move into deeper and deeper belief in God. The goal is to help you see all of life through the lens of the gospel and to live according to that belief and grow in speaking the gospel to others. But as with anything, you'll only get out of it what you put into it.

This first reflection builds a foundation for the rest of the *Handbook* by asking you to be 100% honest with God and with yourself. What struggles and battles, what lies and accusations, what temptations or words from the past pull you away from trusting in God and believing his gospel? In other words, what are some areas of personal unbelief?

To help get the ball rolling, here are some examples that Jeff listed in chapter 1 of *Gospel Fluency*:

- "I have a conversation with my wife, and when she points out something I've yet to get better at, I hear the word *failure* in my head."

- "I try to lead a good conversation about the Bible at the dinner table with my children, but instead of eager beavers on the edges of their seats, I get slouched bodies and rolling eyes. *Bad father.*"

- I teach on being a good neighbor, one who knows the stories of the people who live on your street, but since I moved into my current neighborhood a few months ago, I know only the story of failed attempts to meet people. *Hypocrite.*"

What are 3-5 situations in your own life and the specific lies/accusations/unbeliefs revealed by each?

4. As you look back at those lies and areas of unbelief, remember—and pray that God will help you believe and rest in—this truth: "God wants to rescue you from unbelief and sanctify you to become like Jesus. *Sanctification* is just a big word for becoming more and more *like* Jesus through faith *in* Jesus. You *become like* what you *believe in.* So becoming like Jesus requires believing in Jesus more and more in every part of your life. Sanctification is moving from unbelief in Jesus to belief in Jesus in the everyday stuff of life."

Give Them Jesus

WEEK 1, READING 2

Thoughtfully read the following excerpts, or for more context and a deeper dive, read chapter 2 of *Gospel Fluency*.

The apostle Paul, in his letter to the church in Ephesus, states: "And he gave the apostles, the prophets, the evangelists, the shepherds and teachers, to equip the saints for the work of ministry, for building up the body of Christ, until we all attain to the unity of the faith and of the knowledge of the Son of God, to mature manhood, to the measure of the stature of the fullness of Christ, so that we may no longer be children, tossed to and fro by the waves and carried about by every wind of doctrine, by human cunning, by craftiness in deceitful schemes. *Rather, speaking the truth in love, we are to grow up in every way into him who is the head, into Christ*" (Eph. 4:11–15, *italics added*).

It is God's intent that every person who comes into a relationship with him through Jesus Christ eventually grows up into maturity. And maturity looks like Jesus. He is the perfect human, providing an example of what we are meant to be. A mature Christian is one who resembles Jesus Christ in thought, attitude, emotion, and behavior. And one of the most significant ways by which we grow up into maturity is by speaking the truth in love to each other.

Many wrongly believe that speaking the truth in love is actually just speaking hard words to each other with loving hearts: "You have bad breath, but since I love you, I've got to speak the truth to you." "We want you in our group, but you aren't very kind to others, and as a result, people don't want to be around you! I'm just speaking the truth in love." But that is not what Paul is talking about here. Sure, we do need to speak truthfully to one another, and do it with love for each other, but Paul has something more in mind.

We need to read just a few verses further to discover what Paul means. He clarifies the truth that we are to speak to each other in verse 21. He states, "The truth is in Jesus." "Speaking the truth in love," for Paul, is shorthand for "speaking what is true about Jesus" to one another—that is, speaking the gospel to one another. Paul knows that if people are going to grow up *into* Christ in *every* way, they need to hear the *truths* of Jesus (the gospel) and learn to speak them *into everything*.

Too often, when giving people answers to their questions or solutions to their problems, we give them something other than Jesus. If they are struggling with their finances, we give them the best budgeting plans we know of. If they are working through relational discord, we teach them communication techniques. If they are struggling with doubt, we challenge them to just believe, promising that all will get better if they do. But we fail if we don't give them Jesus.

In some cases, we encourage them to read their Bibles or pray, which, of course, are wonderful things. However, if we don't teach them to meet and know Jesus through their Bible reading and prayer, we are dangerously close to leading them away from Jesus through very good things. This is the heart of idolatry—taking a good thing and making it a "god thing." We take something God gave us to direct us to him and love it or depend on it more than him. As a result, we fail to come to him through it.

I have met too many people who love their Bibles yet have no genuine relationship with Jesus Christ. They don't really know him. They don't really love him. They don't worship him. Instead, they worship their Bibles. They are not growing up into maturity because they are not growing up into Christ.

. . . If we fail to give each other Jesus, we lead each other away from Jesus. We might grow in Bible knowledge, but not in love for Jesus. We might become the most religious pray-ers of all and yet be talking to the wrong god. We could have our finances in order while our hearts are completely out of order because we are doing it all for the wrong reasons. We might be great at communication and conflict resolution, but if we are not reconciled with God through Jesus Christ, then our relationships will be shallow and temporary in nature.

Think of it this way—if we are to help one another grow up into Christ in every way, we need to learn how to speak the truths of Christ into everything—every aspect of life, every situation we face, and every issue we address. This is gospel fluency.

Thoughtfully read the following passages of Scripture related to today's theme. Take a few moments to write down words and phrases that particularly struck you, as well as any thoughts or personal applications they prompted. Make these words a prayer to God.

John 3:16, 5:39-40

Romans 5:8, 8:32

Ephesians 4:1-32

Give Them Jesus

WEEK 1, REFLECTION 2

To apply the concepts of this week's "Reading #2" in your everyday life, pray that God will open your eyes and guide you, then answer the following questions and complete the exercises.

1. Considering the content you read, how would you define speaking the truth in love (Eph. 4:15)?

2. Here's the context of Paul's exhortation to "speak the truth in love": "And [God] gave the apostles, the prophets, the evangelists, the shepherds and teachers, to equip the saints for the work of ministry, for the building up of the body of Christ, until we attain to the unity of the faith and of the knowledge of the Son of God, to mature manhood, to the measure of the stature of the fullness of Christ, so that we may no longer be children, tossed to and fro by the waves and carried about by every wind of doctrine, by human cunning, by craftiness in deceitful schemes. Rather, speaking the truth in love, we are to grow up in every way into him who is the head, into Christ . . ." (Eph. 4:11-15).

Reflect on this passage and the contrast Paul builds between maturity and childhood, as you answer the following questions:

○ The goal of v.11's various gifts and perspectives is to help other followers of Jesus grow into maturity. What specific phrases does Paul use to describe the maturity for which the body (God's Church) is "equipped" and "built up"?

○ Consider each of the "childish" ways Paul lists that people try and grow in Christ: why does each fail us?

- "Tossed to and fro by the waves": what are some of life's waves that can capsize your belief and hinder your growth in Christ?

- "Every wind of doctrine": how does mere mental ascent to biblical truths—without a stirred affection for the God those truths reveal—hinder your growth in Christ?

- "Human cunning": how can trust in yourself, your abilities, and your objective view of life, faith, and God, all let you down as you pursue growth in Christ?

- "Craftiness in deceitful schemes": What are some ways that you've been taught or encouraged to grow in Christ— maybe even by well-meaning Christian leaders—other than a deepening belief in the gospel of Jesus? How do those ways fail you?

- Considering Paul's comment that as we receive "truth in love, we are to grow up *in every way* . . . into Christ" (italics added), what are some areas of life and faith that God has gifted you with belief and maturity? What are some areas of life and faith that you feel weaker and prone to disbelief? It's in these areas that God's "truth in love" might be most helpful at this point in your personal life and growth in Christ.

3. In chapter 2 of *Gospel Fluency*, Jeff modeled "speaking truth in love" into specific areas of Alisa's unbelief: "'Alisa,' I said, 'Jesus is the only man who will never let you down. Every other man will fail you, but he never will. God wants you to stop looking to your ex-husband, or any other man for that matter, to be for you what only Jesus can be for you. He wants Jesus to be at the center of your heart, your affections, and your hope. Jesus wants you to know that he loves you very much and wants to be your ultimate protector and provider…

'Well, God loved you so much that he sent his only Son to die on the cross for your sins. While you were an enemy of God, God loved you enough to die for you so that you can be forgiven. You can be certain that he will provide for you. If he didn't hold back his only Son, you can be certain he will give you every other good gift that you need as well.

'And not only does he love you and want to provide for you,' I continued, 'but he also wants to set you free from the past. Jesus suffered for sin—your sin and the sin of others—so that you not only might be forgiven yourself, but also be able to forgive others and be healed of the wounds you've received through the sins done against you. God wants you to come to him through faith in Jesus for forgiveness and healing.

'We can eventually talk to your ex-husband if you'd like, but what is most important is that you meet Jesus, come to know his love for you, and be healed by him yourself. What is most important is that Jesus becomes the center of your life instead of your ex-husband or anything else. God alone can forgive and provide what you really need, and love you forever through what Jesus has done for you.'"

Look back at the areas of unbelief you identified in this week's Reflection #1. In what ways does God provide an answer to each area, specifically through the person and work of Jesus? It's okay if you don't fully know; you may ask a friend, or you may spend some time in the Bible or in prayer, asking God to show you truths of the gospel. For areas of gospel truth you do know, write a few words like those mentioned above, "speaking" truth to the specific areas of unbelief you wrote down:

4. As you look back at the truths you applied to those areas of unbelief, remember—and pray that God will help you believe and rest in—this truth: "Jesus is the true and better human, and everything in life is better if Jesus is brought into it. He has done everything better. He can make everything better. And the truths about who he is and what he has done, when applied to our lives, are always a better answer than anything else. There is good news and great help for absolutely everything in life in the person and work of Jesus Christ." Consider writing out your thoughts and prayers as you reflect.

Fluency

WEEK 1, READING 3

Thoughtfully read the following excerpts, or for more context and a deeper dive, read chapter 3 of *Gospel Fluency*.

I have found that most Christians don't really know why we need the gospel, what it is, why it is good news, and what it actually does—at least not enough to apply it to the everyday stuff of life. It's not that they *can't* know it well, but most aren't being equipped to become gospel-fluent people. Most believers have become gospel-snippet people, who speak gospel catchphrases. They're speaking gospel-ish, but not the actual gospel in a way people can hear and believe. They say: "Well, we preached the gospel, but they rejected it. People just have hard hearts and deaf ears" . . .

I'm not sure that we should just write ourselves an excuse when we preach what we believe is "good news." It may not be good news to our hearers if we don't take time to listen, understand, and then speak the gospel to the real brokenness and longing of their souls in a way that they can hear—a way that sounds like the good news of Jesus for them and their present situations. We must do better at this.

You gain fluency in a language when you move from merely translating an unfamiliar language into a familiar one to interpreting all of life through that new language. It happens when you can think, feel, and speak in a language. In a sense, the new language becomes the filter through which you perceive the world and help others perceive your world and theirs.

I spent the second semester of my junior year in college studying in Spain to fulfill my language requirement. Prior to leaving Michigan, I took a crash course in Spanish, learning some basic grammar and common phrases. [Once in Spain] I lived in a home where my host mom knew no English. Some of my professors spoke only Spanish, and the majority of the people in the town where I lived were unable to speak English at all. For the first month, I went to bed exhausted every night. Communication was tiresome. I had to listen very closely to people as they spoke Spanish (way too fast at first), process every word and phrase, translate into English, think about what I wanted to say in English, translate that back into Spanish in my head, and then speak it while trying to remember how to maneuver my mouth to say every word correctly. It was exhausting! So, during this time, I learned to listen a lot and talk very little, because talking was just too tiring.

After a few months of being immersed in constant Spanish for every moment—hearing it every-

where I went, reading it on every sign, listening to radio and television broadcasts in Spanish, and speaking it most of the day—I woke up one morning realizing I had been dreaming in Spanish. Something had changed. It became more normative for me to see something and describe it in my head with Spanish words and ideas . . . Gradually, I stopped translating every word and phrase because I started thinking in Spanish. I was becoming more fluent.

I believe this is what God wants his people to experience with the gospel. He wants them to be able to translate the world around them and the world inside of them through the lens of the gospel— the truths of God revealed in the person and work of Jesus. Gospel-fluent people think, feel, and perceive everything in light of what has been accomplished in the person and work of Jesus Christ.

They see the world differently. They think differently. They feel differently. Most significantly, those who are growing in gospel fluency are experiencing ongoing transformation themselves. They are experiencing ongoing change as the truths of the gospel are brought to bear on their thoughts, beliefs, emotions, and actions, transforming them into greater Christlikeness every day. They are growing up into Christ in every way because they are learning to hear and speak the truths of Jesus Christ into everything.

You *do* need to receive some formal training in the basics of the gospel, just as learning a language requires knowing the basics of grammar, vocabulary, and sentence structure . . . However, formal training alone does not make one fluent.

You become fluent through immersion in a gospel-speaking community and through ongoing practice. You have to know it, regularly hear it, and practice proclaiming it.

Language fluency requires immersion into a community of people who speak the language constantly. Gospel fluency requires immersion into a community of people so saturated with the gospel of Jesus Christ that they just can't stop speaking the truths of Jesus wherever they go and in whatever situations they find themselves.

Thoughtfully read the following passages of Scripture related to today's theme. Take a few moments to write down words and phrases that particularly struck you, as well as any thoughts or personal applications they prompted. Make these words a prayer to God.

1 Corinthians 1:18, 2:14

Ephesians 1:22–23, 4:15

Colossians 1:15–20

Fluency

WEEK 1, REFLECTION 3

To apply the concepts of this week's "Reading #3" in your everyday life, pray that God will open your eyes and guide you, then answer the following questions and complete the exercises.

1. Considering all the content you've read this week, how would you define "gospel fluency"?

2. Considering "Reading #3," what are some examples of "gospelish" you've experienced in your own life? In what ways are they different than, and insufficient for, true "gospel immersion"?

3. In today's reading, Jeff writes, "[God] wants [his people] to be able to translate the world around them and the world inside of them through the lens of the gospel—the truths of God revealed in the person and work of Jesus. Gospel-fluent people think, feel, and perceive everything in light of what has been accomplished in the person and work of Jesus Christ.

"They see the world differently. They think differently. They feel differently.

"When they are listening to people, they are thinking: 'How is this in line with the truths of the gospel? What about Jesus and his work might be good news to this person today? How can I bring the hope of the gospel to bear on this life or situation so this person might experience salvation and Jesus will be glorified?'"

The Apostle Paul encourages followers of Jesus to "walk in wisdom toward outsiders [those who aren't followers of Jesus], making the best use of the time. Let your speech always be gracious, seasoned with salt, so that you may know how you ought to answer each person" (Col 4:5-6). Consider this poignant charge, on a few different levels:

- Paul first encourages a life in which followers of Jesus live among those who aren't followers of Jesus. List the names of people in your life who don't follow Jesus, who you'd consider close friends.

O   What are some of the qualities of actual salt that Paul applies to our speaking with those who don't follow Jesus? It may be helpful to answer in light of the posture Peter calls Christians to in 1 Peter 3:15-16.

O   "Answer[ing] each person" connotes personalization. It means there is no single right way to speak the truth of the gospel, whether to yourself, to other Christians, or to those who don't follow Jesus. Consider your own experience:

   •   Among the countless beautiful truths seen in the gospel, which was/were most impactful in the way that God made the gospel real to you in your salvation? (We'll go first: For both of us, we'd known that salvation benefited our eternal lives, but at one point for each of us, God helped us see that the gospel is for every aspect of this life, too. For Jeff it was that Jesus fulfilled a deep longing and brought redemption and healing, after being deeply hurt and angry at all those who had failed to fulfill him; for Ben it was God's promise and proof that Jesus was ultimately satisfying, while he was pursuing satisfaction in many other things that let him down.)

- List some of the truths of the gospel you think might be most impacting **a)** to a few close friends in your Christian community and **b)** to the friends you listed above, who don't yet believe in Jesus.

4. As you look back at your first steps into seeing the world through the lens of the gospel, remember—and pray that God will help you believe and rest in—this truth: "You gain fluency in a language when you move from merely translating an unfamiliar language into a familiar one to interpreting all of life through that new language. It happens when you can think, feel, and speak in a language. In a sense, the new language becomes the filter through which you perceive the world and help others perceive your world and theirs." Consider writing out your thoughts and prayers as you reflect on this truth.

Look Back

After completing your Readings and Reflections, and before your group meets this week, take a few moments to look over your readings and reflections: What have you learned? How has God shaped and impacted you? What do you especially want to remember, do, and/or share with your group this week?

Group Discussion

Looking back over this week's personal readings and reflection, discuss at least one or two of the following questions with a close community of friends. As you discuss, remember your commitment to be honest, and to help each other "grow up in Christ" by "speaking truth in love" with each other.

1. What concepts were new, or especially stood out, from this week's readings? What was difficult from the readings? What questions do you have from the readings?

2. As a group, how would we together define this week's concepts: "unbelief," "speaking the truth in love," and "gospel fluency"?

A key concept from Reading #3 (and chapter 3 of *Gospel Fluency*) is this: "Language fluency requires immersion into a community of people who speak the language constantly. Gospel fluency requires immersion into a community of people so saturated with the gospel of Jesus Christ that they just can't stop speaking the truths of Jesus wherever they go and in whatever situations they find themselves."

3. In what ways does our group reflect this picture of community?

4. In what ways don't we, and why (what barriers, temptations, and lies might exist)?

5. Are there any commitments we can make together in light of this, as we pursue "gospel immersion" together?

6. Apply the gospel, even to this conversation: in what ways do we need the truth and power of God the Father (seen most clearly in the life, death, and resurrection of God the Son, and empowered in us by God the Spirit) to help make us a community that overcomes barriers, talks about Jesus, speaks truth in love to each other, and grows together in Christ?

Group Exercise

Stemming from this week's Personal Readings/Reflections, walk through the following activity as a group. If your group is larger than about six people, you may want to divide into groups of three or four, to make sure everyone gets a chance to participate. Alternatively, one or two people could plan to share their story each week as you walk through the rest of this book. Be real, honest, prayerful, and loving, as you make these truths personal together.

First, have each person...

O   Share one area of unbelief you listed in Reflection #1: take sufficient time to explain the situation, tell the story, and list struggles and battles; lies and accusations; temptations or words from the past, that pull you away from belief in God and his gospel.

O   Either explain ways you applied truth to that area in Reflection #2 (How do you see God provide answers and truth, specifically through the person and work of Jesus?), or if you have a hard time knowing how the gospel provides answers or truth, ask for help.

After each person shares, have others in the group…

○ Celebrate specific ways that God is working in that person's life—sanctifying him/her by bringing his truth to the situation he/she explained. Considering how you shared stories (see "Introduction"), mention themes you noticed of God's work and specific ways you see him drawing each person into deeper belief, relationship, and rest in him through the gospel.

○ Ask questions and speak truth in love to each other. What did you notice as they shared? What gospel themes or ways God is working did you pick up on that might encourage or exhort the person who shared?

NOTE

Enrich your learning and experience for this week by watching the companion video at **saturatetheworld.com/gf**

PRAY

Spend some time praying together, for your group and for each specific person: that God would help you each believe more and more in him and in his gospel work; that he will help apply that truth to your everyday thoughts, words, and actions; and that he will grow you into existing as a community that models and speaks the gospel to each other and to others.

The Gospel

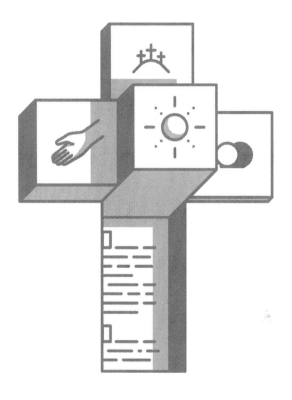

WEEK 2

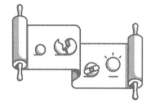

The True Story

WEEK 2, READING 1

Thoughtfully read the following excerpts, or for more context and a deeper dive, read chapter 4 of *Gospel Fluency*.

All of us are living our lives under a dominant story. We perceive the world and human interactions through the stories we know and believe. For most of us, that is our story of origin, our family story. This is a much smaller story inside the larger one, and often it leads us to wrong perceptions of God, ourselves, others, and the world around us. In some cases, we believe outright lies.

But there is a true story. It's the story of God found in the Bible.

It's the story that redeems, heals, and completes our personal stories—the smaller stories within the true story. We will talk about the makeup of the gospel (like vocabulary) and how it has meaning for our lives (like grammar), but we first need to get the overarching story, because it is the true story that informs the meaning of the gospel.

CREATION

"In the beginning God . . ." (Gen. 1:1). That is how the story begins—with God.

God eternally existed in community—God the Father, God the Son, and God the Holy Spirit—one God in three persons, existing in perfect unity. Nothing else existed. In the beginning, God created by his word. He created the heavens and the earth out of nothing. He spoke and it all came into being. God's word brought about God's work. The questions "Who am I?" and "Why am I here?" are not meant to be answered outside of what God says and what God does. Before we go any further, ask yourself: "Who or what do I look to—trust in, depend upon—for my worth?"

God called the man to trust him and obey him: "Believe who I say you are. Trust in what I've done to make you who you are. And as a result, do what I command". . . [Genesis 1 and 2 display a picture of perfect Creation]: a mandate to love, work, and rule in such a way as to show all of creation what God is like. A good and beautiful garden. A man and woman living in harmonious and pure love, naked and unashamed, daily enjoying each other, working and ruling over creation, and interacting with God in their midst. It was all very good! But that was about to change.

FALL

They didn't believe. They didn't trust God's word and work. The problem was unbelief. The action was sin. The result was death. The Serpent, the Devil, convinced the woman that God's word was a lie and his work was not good: "God knows you aren't as good as you could be. He knows that if you just took matters into your own hands, you would be much better. You can be like God if you just eat the fruit of the tree he told you not to eat of." She believed the lie and ate the fruit; then she gave some to her husband, and he ate too.

God had told them they were very good—they were made in his image, after his likeness. But they didn't believe him. Instead, they believed the Devil, the master of lies. God had told them they would surely die if they ate the fruit. But they didn't believe him. Instead, they believed the lie of the Devil, that they wouldn't die. As a result of their rebellion, sin entered the world and brought about death and destruction. The wages of sin *is* death—spiritual, relational, and physical. Sinful rebellion produces brokenness, suffering, and death. This is because rebellion against God is rebellion against the giver of life. And this rebellion began and continues to go on because of unbelief in the truthfulness of God's word and the sufficiency of his work.

REDEMPTION

Thankfully, the story doesn't end with destruction and death. Even as the man and woman were being informed about the curse of sin and its effects on their lives and relationships, God also promised to put an end to the Serpent and the rebellion he had started. Through Eve's offspring, Satan would eventually be crushed (Gen. 3:15). God would have the final word. He would save us from our sin. He would rescue us from Satan. He would put death to death. His word is true and his work is sufficient.

[Adam and Eve had failed. As the Bible unfolds, generation after generation of God's people fail too.] God's plan, however, did not. He would still fulfill his word. Through [Adam and Eve's] offspring, the world would be blessed. Another son—the true Son of God—would accomplish it. Jesus is that Son.

Jesus came as the true and better Adam, the true and better Abraham, and the true and better Israel. God's full and final redemption to rescue us from slavery to sin and Satan came in the form of a baby. He is God's redemption plan. He always was—even before the creation of the world.

NEW CREATION

[After Jesus's death and burial, he] was raised with a glorified body. He took on our sin at the cross, where he paid for it with his blood and destroyed its power. He overcame death and was given new life. And in his glorified, sinless body that can no longer be taken down by Satan, sin, or death, he has been given all authority in heaven and earth. He is the new and better Adam over a new and better creation. The church is Jesus' bride. We are God's new-creation people. All those who believe in Jesus' life, death, and resurrection go from having Adam as their authority and life source to having Jesus as the new Adam. Adam sinned, and everyone born since then was born into sin as a result. Everyone except Jesus.

Everything has changed. Our identity and our purpose, as well as our understanding of the truths of God, have completely changed. We also have a future hope. The new creation is not just personal but cosmic. God will bring about a new heaven and new earth, which we will get to live in and enjoy forever. The true image of God, Jesus, will light up that world with his glory, and we also, with renewed resurrection bodies, will reflect God as redeemed, recreated, and resurrected image bearers, transformed by the glory of Christ.

This is our story. This is *the* story. This is the true and better story that can redeem and make new every other story. You want to change a culture? Give them a new story. Language will follow.

Thoughtfully read the following passages of Scripture related to today's theme. Take a few moments to write down words and phrases that particularly struck you, as well as any thoughts or personal applications they prompted. Make these words a prayer to God.

Genesis 1–3

The True Story

To apply the concepts of this week's "Reading #1" in your everyday life, pray that God will open your eyes and guide you, then answer the following questions and complete the exercises.

1. Considering the content you read, what are the four key movements in the Story of God?

2. Think through various realities in life: from the Scriptures, personal experience, arts, nature, history or personal relationships, what are some ways you see, hear, and experience this story being re-told, over and over again, in everyday life?

3. Zoom in a bit: **a)** In the first column below, write some of the ways that each movement of the Story of God can display and remind us of God's hope and design for his people. **b)** In the second column, write some of the ways that each movement can point us specifically toward Jesus.

	GOD'S DESIGN FOR HIS PEOPLE	POINTS ME TO JESUS
CREATION		
FALL		
REDEMPTION		
NEW CREATION		

In chapter four of *Gospel Fluency*, Jeff uses the image of a father to display the various ways our own stories define or redefine our worldview.

> *"All of us are living our lives under a dominant story. We perceive the world and human interactions through the stories we know and believe. For most of us, that is our story of origin, our family story. This is a much smaller story inside the larger one, and often it leads us to wrong perceptions of God, ourselves, others, and the world around us. In some cases, we believe outright lies."*

If we don't view life through the lens of God's story, we view it in light of a lesser story.

In the first column below, we've listed the dominant questions asked by each movement of God's story. In the second column, we've listed some of

	QUESTION	OBJECTIVE/BIBLICAL ANSWER
CREATION	Where is my identity? What do I look to, trust in, depend on, for my worth?	Child of God, created in his image; my identity is in Christ alone; I am reliant/dependent on him
FALL	What is wrong here? What is the real problem/issue?	Sin Rejection of God Brokenness that's part of living in a fallen world
REDEMPTION	What can fix this? What will make this right?	Jesus
NEW CREATION	Where is hope? In what is my confidence found?	God's promises shown through history Eternity/Jesus' return

the objective, biblical answers to those questions which come when God's story is our dominant story. In the third column, re-write a few of the areas of disbelief you struggle with. In the final column, consider alternative narratives that reinforce this area of unbelief. What is the story you are believing instead of the story of God?

> *NOTE: If you didn't pick areas in Week 1, or if it would help you to start with less personal areas of disbelief, choose some common areas of disbelief in peoples' everyday lives. Here are a few starting points (from chapter 3 of *Gospel Fluency*): "We are Jesus's people, who speak the truths of Jesus into the everyday stuff of life. Speak the truths of Jesus to rightly order our budgets. Speak the truths of Jesus for finding a spouse. Speak the truths of Jesus for how we respond to our employers or employees. Speak the truths of Jesus for how we parent our children. Speak the truths of Jesus into everything." (For more practice in this, download the following chart at **saturatetheworld.com/gf**. Pick various areas of life and ask/answer the same questions.)

AREA OF DISBELIEF	POSSIBLE "FALSE" ANSWERS/STORY

4. It may feel like stopping here brought you to a low point, without reminding you of hope. We promise: Readings and Reflections #2 and 3 will bring you out of that pit. But as you compare God's objective story to the lesser stories that can dominate our worldview, remember—and pray that God will help you believe and rest in—this truth: "The new creation has already begun in Jesus and is real and begun in us, and one day he will bring it to full completion. Until then, we live as the redeemed people of God, becoming more and more like Jesus every day so that more and more people come to him through our visible and verbal testimony. This is our story. This is *the* story. This is the true and better story that can redeem and make new every other story." Consider writing out your thoughts and prayers as you reflect on this truth.

Power for Salvation

WEEK 2, READING 2

Thoughtfully read the following excerpts, or for more context and a deeper dive, read chapter 5 of *Gospel Fluency*.

When people say they are *saved*, what do they mean? Think of this chapter as a vocabulary lesson. To become fluent in any language, you must develop your vocabulary. So let's delve into the aspects of the gospel that are expressed in the person and work of Jesus more fully.

Belief in the gospel is not a one-time decision or a conviction that we need salvation only for our past lives and future afterlives. Belief in the gospel is an ongoing expression of our ongoing need for Jesus. The gospel is the power of God for salvation to all who *believe* (Rom. 1:16). What do we believe? What are we putting our faith in?

Jesus' life represents both the righteousness of God in human form and the perfect fulfillment of the standard of righteousness on behalf of humanity. If you want to know what the righteousness of God looks like, you look at Jesus' life, and if you want to be declared righteous by God, you need to have faith in how Jesus lived on your behalf, not just in how he died. We all needed a new human to give birth to a new humanity—a perfect man who is also the true image of God, fully displaying what God is like by living a fully submitted and obedient life before God. Jesus is that man. "He is the image of the invisible God, the firstborn of all creation" (Col. 1:15). We need more than the humble life of Christ. We also need the victorious rule and ministry of Christ to overcome Satan's schemes, bring healing and restoration to the brokenness that sin produces, and provide reconciliation between God and man.

Jesus was betrayed, arrested, wrongly accused, and crucified. The perfect Son of God, the righteousness of God, the one who knew no sin, became sin at the cross so that we might become the righteousness of God in him. We needed a perfect substitute—one without sin, fully pleasing to God—who would die in our place. The Bible says, "For the wages of sin is death, but the free gift of God is eternal life in Christ Jesus our Lord" (Rom. 6:23). Our sin, our rebellion, every way in which we fall short of the glory of God, were put on Jesus at the cross. His perfect life was exchanged for our life of sin. Jesus died for our sins. He took our sins on himself—on his real physical, human body—and then died for them. Our sins were buried with Jesus. They were not just

removed and put in another place. They were destroyed by his death. If your faith is in Jesus, your sins, past, present, and future, were terminated through Jesus' death.

[Jesus] was raised on the third day and appeared to more than five hundred people. He was raised with a glorified body, one without sin. This was a body for the new creation. The gospel doesn't just bring about forgiveness of sins and save us from hell. The gospel of Jesus Christ empowers us to live a whole new life today by the same Spirit who raised Jesus from the dead. After Jesus rose from the dead, he ascended to the right hand of God the Father, where he is now making intercession on our behalf. He is continually praying for us, willing to empower us by his Spirit in us, and speaking a better word over us than Satan, sin, or our past experiences speak.

After Jesus' resurrection and ascension, God sent his Spirit to wake us up from spiritual death, convict us of our sin, make the truths of the gospel clear to our hearts, grant us repentance and faith, and bring about new life as a result. By his Spirit, we are born again from the dead, spiritually speaking. We become new creations in Christ. Each of us has a new nature, a new identity, and a new purpose. And the Spirit in those who believe is a sign of all of this. The Spirit is also the means by which we have the power to live entirely new and different lives. He is the sign that we are forgiven and cleansed, changed and made new, chosen and adopted by God—he wants us, he chose us, he changed us, he empowers us, and he loves us.

All of this is a gift. It is all by grace. "For by grace you have been saved through faith. And this is not your own doing; it is the gift of God, not a result of works, so that no one may boast (Eph. 2:8–9).

Thoughtfully read the following passages of Scripture related to today's theme. Take a few moments to write down words and phrases that particularly struck you, as well as any thoughts or personal applications they prompted. Make these words a prayer to God.

Mark 1:9-11

Romans 1:16-17, 3:21-26, 8:9-17

1 Corinthians 15:1-6, 15:20-23

2 Corinthians 5:16-21

Philippians 2:6-8

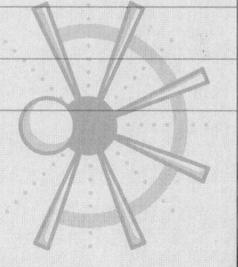

Power for Salvation

WEEK 2, REFLECTION 2

To apply the concepts of this week's "Reading #2" in your everyday life, pray that God will open your eyes and guide you, then answer the following questions and complete the exercises.

1. Considering the content you read, define "salvation," and explain what it is Christians believe we're saved from?

2. What stands out to you, or particularly strikes you, as you consider the life, death, and resurrection of Jesus?

3. In your own words, explain why each following element matters in general, and why each is vital to your understanding of the concept of salvation? (*NOTE: If the theological words below are new, unfamiliar, or confusing, they're briefly defined in the **Appendix**, page 268.*)

- Jesus' life (think through various biblical truths regarding Jesus' life on earth, and especially consider Jesus' obedience, sinlessness, baptism, humility, Spirit-ledness, and kingship)

- Jesus' death (think through various biblical truths regarding Jesus' death, and especially consider the substitution, atonement, forgiveness, and propitiation offered through his death)

- Jesus' resurrection (think through various biblical truths regarding Jesus' resurrection, and especially his bodily resurrection, his ascension, and his sending of God the Spirit)

4. "Jesus died in our place to save us from the wrath of God and the penalty of sin, which is spiritual, relational, and physical death. He saves us from spiritual death and makes us alive in Christ. He atones for our guilt and removes our shame. He reconciles us to God so that we can also be reconciled to one another. And ultimately, though our bodies will fail and die, he will give us glorified resurrection bodies that will live forever."

    Look back at the "possible false answers/stories" you wrote down in Reflection #1. In essence, if we're finding our answers in any place but God—and the objective, biblical answers he gives to our questions—we're pursuing a false savior. Take some time and compare and contrast the possible false answers you wrote earlier this week to the implications of Jesus' life, death, and resurrection you wrote in today's Reflection. Where does each story find its power? What does each story promise? Historically, how has each proven to fulfill promises or let you down?

POTENTIAL POWER IN OTHER STORIES	ACTUAL POWER IN JESUS (LIFE/DEATH/RESURRECTION)

5. As you consider the power of Jesus' life, death, and resurrection, and the power found therein for salvation and growth, end with—and pray that God will help you believe and rest in—this truth: **"The gospel is the good news of the life, death, burial, and resurrection of Jesus, who is King. The gospel saves and brings God's rule into our lives (his kingdom) in order to bring the good news of his power into the world. The gospel changes us from the inside out and spreads through our lives and lips to the world by his Spirit. This is the gospel that is the power of God for salvation to all who believe."** Consider writing out your thoughts and prayers as you reflect on this truth.

What's Faith Got to Do with It?

WEEK 2, READING 3

Thoughtfully read the following excerpts, or for more context and a deeper dive, read chapter 6 of *Gospel Fluency*.

We all live by faith in someone or something. And everything that we are and do is a result of what we believe. Our behaviors are the tangible expression of our beliefs. It is by grace you have been saved through faith . . . A gospel-fluent community that is growing in faith in the gospel is evidenced by people confessing their sins to one another regularly . . . A gospel-fluent community that is growing in confidence that Jesus fully atoned for our sins extends grace and forgiveness to one another. It is by grace—the gift of God in Jesus—that you are saved from the consequences and control of sin. And it is through faith—belief in Jesus' work on our behalf. Every sinful attitude, motive, thought, or action is a result of unbelief in God's word and work.

Paul teaches in Romans 1:18–32 that we all, like Adam and Eve and all their descendants, have exchanged the truth of God for a lie and have worshiped the creation instead of the Creator. We put our faith in the things God has made or the things we can do instead of God. God gives us over to our wrong belief and lets it produce in us what all idolatry produces—sin, brokenness, perversion, and pain.

He does this so that we will see the wretchedness of sin and turn back to him as the one who forgives our sin, cleanses us from unrighteousness, and heals our brokenness.

The gospel is not just the power of God to save, but also the revelation of God that we need to be saved and that the only one who can save us is Jesus. The Spirit's job is to reveal to us our unbelief, grant us repentance, and lead us to know and believe in Jesus. That is the work we do. We turn from unbelief to belief in Jesus. Unbelief can take several forms: **1)** we don't believe because we lack the truth about God; **2)** we believe lies about God; **3)** we fail to put our faith in what we know to be true of God; or **4)** we've been wounded and need healing.

First, many don't know who God really is. They don't know what he is like or what he has done for us. A person can't believe in God if he or she is unaware of the truths about God. There is no salvation—no transformation—apart from knowing God. One of the reasons Jesus came—and one of the reasons why the gospel is such good news— was to reveal the truth about God and to bring us into relationship with him. In the gospel, we have the revelation of what God is like and what God has done. God is revealed through Jesus' life, Jesus' ministry, Jesus' death, and Jesus' resurrection. What is your God like? What do you believe about God? Growing in gospel fluency requires growing in our knowledge of God as he is revealed in and through Jesus Christ.

Second, in some cases, our unbelief involves believing lies about God. Satan deceived Adam and Eve into believing lies about God, and we regularly buy into his lies as well. We might know certain truths about God, but fail to believe those truths because we are deceived into believing lies. Jesus came to dispel the lies. Regularly, we hear Jesus say, "Truly, truly I say . . ." He is replacing the lies we believe with the truths of God. Not only does he proclaim those truths verbally, but he is also the ultimate example and display of those truths. Growing in gospel fluency requires regularly replacing lies we have believed with the truths of God revealed in Jesus. One of the reasons God sent his Spirit to us is to reveal the lies and help us believe the truth about God. I regularly invite God's

Spirit to do this in my life. You can too.

Third, we often say we believe something to be true about God, but our lives show that we don't actually believe it. We know a truth we should believe, but in actuality, we don't. For instance, we profess belief in a God who forgives our sins through faith in the death of Jesus, but we continue to believe we need to behave better in order to make up for what we've done. When we do this, we are living in unbelief in the gospel. The gospel is the power of God to save us not only because our sin of unbelief is forgiven through Jesus' death on the cross, but also because in the gospel we come to know and believe the liberating truths of God revealed in Jesus Christ. And through believing those truths, the lies we've believed are dispelled and the truth sets us free to really live.

Finally, for some of us, disbelief isn't primarily an issue of knowing, believing, or repenting. Some of us struggle with the things of God because we've been wounded, and healing is needed as we consider what faith looks like. In the gospel, God offers people forgiveness, eternity, adoption, and many other blessings. But the gospel also promises that "by his wounds you have been healed" (1 Peter 2:24). Without faith, we can often operate out of our flesh. Without healing, we can easily operate out of our brokenness. That brokenness might drive us toward sinful thoughts and behaviors. If this theme resonates with you, know that whatever happened—whatever burden you're carrying and whatever pain you've experienced—Jesus is sufficient. As one who was despised and rejected, mocked, beaten, and killed, there is no wound so deep that Jesus cannot relate; there is no pain so large that God cannot heal; there is no heart so broken that the Spirit cannot help and comfort. God is good, and he extends healing to you. Through the gospel, Christ's wounds heal us. We believe the gospel when we invite God's healing into our brokenness.

So what do you believe? The gospel won't fluently come out of you to others unless it's changed you first.

Thoughtfully read the following passages of Scripture related to today's theme. Take a few moments to write down words and phrases that particularly struck you, as well as any thoughts or personal applications they prompted. Make these words a prayer to God.

John 6:28-29

John 14:1-14

Romans 1:18-32

Romans 3:22-25

Col. 1:15-19

Eph. 2:1-10

James 2:17

What's Faith Got to Do With It?

WEEK 2, REFLECTION 3

To apply the concepts of this week's "Reading #3" in your everyday life, pray that God will open your eyes and guide you, then answer the following questions and complete the exercises.

1. Considering the content you read, define "faith," specifically as it relates to God.

2. Jeff writes in chapter 6 of *Gospel Fluency*, "Tim Chester, in his book *You Can Change*, asserts that underlying every sinful behavior and negative emotion is a failure to believe a truth about God. He then suggests four liberating truths as a good diagnostic tool for addressing sin in our lives:

    O **God is great**—so we do not have to be in control.

    O **God is glorious**—so we do not have to fear others.

    O **God is good**—so we do not have to look elsewhere.

    O **God is gracious**—so we do not have to prove ourselves.[1]

---

1. Tim Chester, You Can Change: God's Transforming Power for Our Sinful Behavior and Negative Emotions (Wheaton, IL: Crossway, 2010), 80.

"Let's take the first as an example: If we believe God is great—that he is in control—then we can trust him and be free from the need to take control or manipulate situations. On the other hand, if we feel anxious or have an urge to take control, it is because we have believed the lie that God is not great—that he's not really powerful and in control—so we have to be. In the gospel, we see just how great God is as he overcomes every enemy we face, including death.

"Jesus came to dispel the lies. Regularly, we hear Jesus say, 'Truly, truly I say . . .' He is replacing the lies we believe with the truths of God. Not only does he proclaim those truths verbally, but he is also the ultimate example and display of those truths."

Looking back at the areas of unbelief you've been wrestling with since Week 1, and the various readings and reflections, is there one "theme" that seems to be central to your difficulty? If you can, identify which of the four truths is, in general, the most difficult for you to regularly believe about God. (It's OK if there's more than one.)

3. "Unbelief can take several forms: **1)** we don't believe because we lack the truth about God (we don't know what God is like or what he has done for us); **2)** we believe lies about God (our unbelief involves believing lies about God); or **3)** we fail to put our faith in what we know to be true of God (we believe something to be true about God, but our lives show that we don't actually believe it)."

Look back at the areas of unbelief you've been working through over these past couple weeks. For each one, can you identify one of these three forms as the source of your unbelief? Write a few of the areas of unbelief, and put a check in the box (or boxes) you feel might be its source. In preparation for your Group Discussion, use the right column to prayerfully write any questions or thoughts it might be helpful to work through when you meet your community this week.

AREA OF UNBELIEF	SOURCE?	QUESTIONS/NOTES TO DISCUSS
	DON'T KNOW	
	BELIEVE LIES	
	LIFE DOESN'T DISPLAY BELIEF	
	DON'T KNOW	
	BELIEVE LIES	
	LIFE DOESN'T DISPLAY BELIEF	
	DON'T KNOW	
	BELIEVE LIES	
	LIFE DOESN'T DISPLAY BELIEF	

4. As this week ends, and before our *Handbook* takes a more practical turn, we pause again to consider the answer to our every unbelief: "grace through faith" in the person and work of Jesus Christ*. That's the power of the gospel; that's the climax of God's true, best story. Read—and pray that God will help you believe and rest in—this truth: "The gospel is the power of God to save us not only because our sin of unbelief is forgiven through Jesus' death on the cross, but also because in the gospel we come to know and believe the liberating truths of God revealed in Jesus Christ. And through believing those truths, the lies we've believed are dispelled and the truth sets us free to really live." Consider writing out your thoughts and prayers as you reflect. (*If the term, "grace through faith" is new or confusing to you, see Appendix A for explanation.)

Look Back

After completing your Readings and Reflections, and before your group meets this week, take a few moments to look over your readings and reflections: What have you learned? How has God shaped and impacted you? What do you especially want to remember, do, and/or share with your group this week?

Group Discussion

Looking back over this week's personal readings and reflection, discuss at least one or two of the following questions with a close community of friends. As you discuss, remember your commitment to be honest, and to help each other "grow up in Christ" by "speaking truth in love" with each other.

1. What concepts were new, or especially stood out, from this week's readings? What was difficult from the readings? What questions do you have from the readings?

2. As a group, how would we together describe the four movements of the *Story of God*, and define this week's concepts: "salvation" and "faith"?

As we consider elements of this week's "basics course" on gospel fluency, we're left with this truth from Reading #3 (and chapter 6 of *Gospel Fluency*): "Growing in gospel fluency requires regularly replacing lies we have believed with the truths of God revealed in Jesus. One of the reasons God sent his Spirit to us is to reveal the lies and help us believe the truth about God. I regularly invite God's Spirit to do this in my life. You can too."

The simple fact is that each of us has blind spots as we consider our own lives and relationships with God: those blind spots are often magnified in areas of sin and disbelief.

3. Has anyone's definition of "gospel fluency" changed over this week? How has it deepened/expanded?

4. Reflection #3 asked you to define potential sources of unbelief: "**1)** . . . we don't believe because we lack the truth about God; **2)** we believe lies about God; or **3)** we fail to put our faith in what we know to be true of God." For areas that could be defined, is there anything we can talk about to help point you toward belief and help you see how the gospel applies to those specific areas of unbelief?

5. Practice applying the gospel together, even to this conversation: If anyone in your community had difficulty with any Reflections, it wouldn't be uncommon for that to stem from areas of unbelief. Ask if anyone had a hard time with anything this week. Then as a group committed to using your God-given gifts, perspective, etc. for "the building up of the body of Christ," take some time to ask questions, recall themes and history from each other's previously shared stories, and help each other "replace lies we have believed with the truths of God revealed in Jesus." There isn't a "right answer" or one way to do this; it's simply a way to help you start to get comfortable speaking the gospel into real-life situations, together.

6. As stated at the beginning of this week, even though you've worked through belief in the gospel from several different angles this week, you'll still need practice, practice, practice. Are there any commitments your group needs to make to each other as you pursue "regularly rehearsing the gospel" in each other's lives together?

Group Exercise

Stemming from this week's conversation related to the Story of God, walk through the following activity as a group. If your group is larger than about six people, you may want to divide into groups of three or four, to make sure everyone gets a chance to participate. Be real, honest, prayerful, and loving, as you make these truths personal together.

First, have each person...

O Pick one of the following stories from the Bible. If you don't know the story itself, read it from the provided scripture references.

- **The story of Adam and Eve** (Genesis 2–3)
- **The story of Cain and Abel** (Genesis 4)
- **The story of Noah and his family** (Genesis 6–9)
- **The story of Abram and his sons** (Genesis 16–18, 21)
- **The story of Jacob and Esau** (Genesis 26–27, 31–33)
- **The story of Joseph and his brothers** (Genesis 37–50)

*NOTE: These stories were chosen because they're all contained within the first book of the Bible. We could go on and on as the Bible unfolds, because this story is literally told over and over again.

O In your own words, summarize the story in light of the four movements of the Story of God: Creation, Fall, Redemption, and New Creation.

After each person shares, together as a group answer the following questions, either during each movement or after each person finishes telling The Story through the specific story they chose:

O   In what things other than God do his people define their identity, problems, solutions, and hope, in this story?

O   What things are true of the redeemer in each story? What does that tell you about God and the gospel?

○ In what ways does this story as a whole—or each movement within it—foreshadow the overarching version of the same story of the whole Bible, that climaxes with Jesus' death and resurrection?

○ In what ways do you personally identify with the people or situations in the story? Which movement (Creation, Fall, Redemption, or New Creation) sticks out the most to you, and why?

○ If needed, take time to speak truth in love to each other: point each other toward the gospel's application to everyday situations as people share what resonates most with them, celebrate specific areas of belief, or help and exhort others in areas of unbelief.

✱ NOTE ✱

Enrich your learning and experience for this week by watching the companion video at **saturatetheworld.com/gf**

PRAY

Spend some time praying together, for your group and for each specific person: that God would help you see his story play out in everyday moments of your lives and that he will lead you to see it as the story that dominates your worldview; that he will keep Jesus' life, death, and resurrection consistently on your mind throughout each day; and that he increases your faith and draws you more and more toward belief in him, in all things.

The Gospel in Me

PART 1

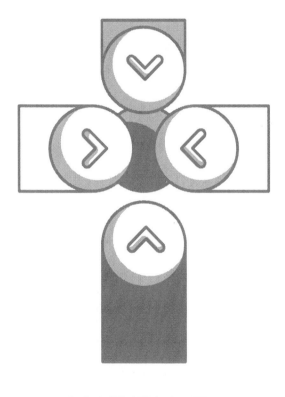

WEEK 3

Weeks 1 and 2 of our journey together focused on the foundation and basics of gospel fluency. Without understanding unbelief itself, and without knowing the Story of God and the power of the gospel, any hope of these concepts becoming real in our lives would be lost. Beginning this week, two things happen. First, if you're reading *Gospel Fluency* rather than the excerpts provided, we slow down from three chapters per week to consider a chapter and a half per week. Second, the rest of the Handbook considers how to apply the concepts of Weeks 1 and 2 to ourselves (Weeks 3 and 4), as a community (Weeks 5 and 6), and as it relates to others (Weeks 7 and 8).

As you might expect from this week's title, "The Gospel in Me" asks you to be introspective: All three Week 3 Readings and Reflections are meant to be "diagnostic"—helping you define specific areas of need for the gospel. Week 4 will focus more on the "remedy," helping give you specific ways to remind yourself of the truths of the gospel, as you grow increasingly fluent over time.

Good News to Me

WEEK 3, READING 1

Thoughtfully read the following excerpts, or for more context and a deeper dive, read the first part of chapter 7 of *Gospel Fluency*, stopping before the section titled "You Talk About What Works."

I'm often asked why it's so hard for many people to talk to others about Jesus . . . I have come to believe that the main reason people don't talk about Jesus isn't that they lack training. I am convinced it is that they lack love. People need heart change—not just once, but over and over again, because their love grows cold. People need to be deeply affected by the incredible news of Jesus on a daily basis. What affects you greatly creates in you great affections. And those affections lead you to express verbally and physically what you love most, because you talk about what you love. Furthermore, you love what you talk about. And we all talk about what most affects us—what most powerfully works to affect change in our lives. Jesus said that it is out of the overflow of the heart that the mouth speaks (Luke 6:45). What comes out of your heart displays what's in it and what has captured it.

Do you talk about Jesus? Has he captured your heart? Do you love him? When you come to know and experience the love God has for us in Jesus; when you realize that God loved us so much that he was willing to suffer and die for our sins, even though we were his enemies; when you meet Jesus and experience him pouring out his Spirit into your heart, filling you with himself and his love, you can't contain it. You have to talk about it! The gospel is incredible! The word gospel literally means "good news." Is it good news to you?

What do you get most excited about? What has most captured your affections? Be honest for a moment. What is it? Who is it? And why has it or he or she captured your heart? And if your affections have been captured, how have you been affected? What do you do in light of your heart being captured?

Most importantly, has Jesus captured your affections? Why or why not? Are you impressed with him? It will show, you know. If he has captured your affections, you will not be able to stop talking about him.

Another reason I talk about Jesus is that I've found you not only talk about what you love, but you also love what you talk about. Sometimes our love grows cold. Our hearts lose affection. We forget what we have, so we drift from what we love.

If you lack love for Jesus and want your love for him to grow, start talking about how amazing he is. Talk to yourself about him. By the way, you won't be alone in this venture because he sent his Spirit to tell you what is true, good, and amazing about Jesus. The Holy Spirit is the best at bragging on Jesus because he has known him forever and is more impressed with him than anyone. Read the Gospels and watch him closely. I would encourage you to read at least one Gospel a year to regularly reacquaint yourself with the love of your life. As you read, slow down and pay attention to his actions and words. Observe how well and how much he loves. Watch for his kindness and gentleness. Don't miss his gracious love for the broken, the weary, and the sinful.

Then, as the Spirit shows you more about Jesus, talk about what you see and learn. Talk to your roommate about how amazing Jesus is.

Tell your friends. Speak with your children about him. The more you do, the more you will love him. And the more you love him, the more you will want to talk about him. Never forget how he loved you first... Regularly go back to that day when his love for you first showed up on the front porch of your heart. Don't forget what it was like when you were first captured by his affection for you. In your thoughts, go back regularly to what life was like without Jesus, then remember how he changed your life forever.

If that has not yet happened to you, if your affections have not yet been captured by Jesus Christ, I pray that will change for you. As it does, tell others about his love. You talk about what you love and you love what you talk about.

Thoughtfully read the following passages of Scripture related to today's theme. Take a few moments to write down words and phrases that particularly struck you, as well as any thoughts or personal applications they prompted. Make these words a prayer to God.

Luke 6:45

John 3:17-21

1 John 4:7-21

Revelation 2:2-7

Good News to Me

WEEK 3, REFLECTION 1

To apply the concepts of this week's "Reading #1" in your everyday life, pray that God will open your eyes and guide you, then answer the following questions and complete the exercises.

1. Considering the content you read, define "love." Additionally, explain why the gospel is regularly called "good news."

2. "What do you get most excited about? What has most captured your affections? Be honest for a moment. What is it? Who is it? And why has it or he or she captured your heart? And if your affections have been captured, how have you been affected? What do you do in light of your heart being captured? Most importantly, has Jesus captured your affections? Why or why not? Are you impressed with him? It will show, you know. If he has captured your affections, you will not be able to stop talking about him."

These questions are similar to those that respected counselor Dr. David Powlison asks in his article, "X-Ray Questions." Originally published in 1999, "each question circles around the same basic issue: Who or what is your functional God/god? Many of the questions simply derive from the verbs that relate you to God: love, trust, fear, hope, seek, obey, take refuge, and the like. Each verb holds out a lamp to guide us to him who is way, truth, and life. But each verb also may be turned into a question, holding up a mirror to show us where we stray. Each question comes at the same general question. In individual situations – different times, places, people—one or another may be more appropriate and helpful. Different ways of formulating the motivation question will ring the bells of different people."[1] Powlison's article includes 35 questions; we've included 10 below. Choose at least five questions to answer honestly, and please don't pretend that your answer to each one is truthfully "Jesus."

- What do you want, desire, crave, lust, and wish for? What desires do you serve and obey?

- What do you seek, aim for, or pursue? What are your goals and expectations?

- What do you fear? What do you want? What do you tend to worry about?

- Where do you find refuge, safety, comfort, escape, pleasure, or security?

- What or who do you trust?

- On your deathbed, what would sum up your life as worthwhile? What gives your life meaning?

---

1. "X-Ray Questions: Drawing Out the Whys and Wherefores of Human Behavior": The Journal of Biblical Counseling • Volume 18 • Number 1 • Fall 1999.

- Whose victory or success would make your life happy? How do you define victory and success?

- What do you see as your rights? What do you feel entitled to?

- How do you spend your time? Who are your priorities?

- What are your characteristic fantasies, either pleasurable or fearful? Daydreams? What do your night dreams revolve around?

3. Think about the things you answered in Question #2: Write a few of them in the left column below. In the middle column, write a few of the reasons that thing is so precious to you. Finally, in the right column, compare each one to Jesus: Are you more impressed with, excited about, and affectionate toward that thing/person, or toward Jesus? Why do you think that is?

WHAT YOU LOVE	WHY YOU LOVE IT	LOVE FOR THAT VS LOVE FOR JESUS

4. What are some of the things that most amaze you, stir your affections for, and excite you about Jesus? What is it about who he is and what he's done in his life, death, and resurrection, that is especially "good news" to you right now? Write down at least five*, and pursue ways in the next few days to share each with someone else—maybe with someone who follows Jesus and someone who doesn't.

   *If this is new to you and you cannot think of specific things you love about Jesus, share that with your community. They have committed to help each other as you journey together through this Handbook. Be honest with them, and ask them to help you with this by remembering your story and pointing out things in your life they think may help stir your affections and excitement for Jesus.

5. As you ponder the person and work of Jesus, and your love for him, read—and pray that God will help you believe and rest in—this truth: "You will talk about [Jesus] if you love him. If you don't, start talking about him, what's he's done, and what he's done for you, and you will love him. And you'll begin to see more and more clearly how wonderful his gospel is and how powerfully it works. As a result, you will talk about Jesus more and more. He is the best news there is." Consider writing out your thoughts and prayers as you reflect.

We Talk About What Works

WEEK 3, READING 2

Thoughtfully read the following excerpts, or for more context and a deeper dive, read the last half of chapter 7 of *Gospel Fluency*, beginning with the section titled "You Talk About What Works."

We like to talk about what is impressive. We talk about what changes us. We talk about what works. We were created by God to work, and in Christ Jesus, we were re-created for good works that God prepared in advance for us to do (Eph. 2:10). This is why we talk about what works. We like things to work. And when things work well, we talk about that. We also talk about what does not work for the same reason.

Now, stop and think again about what you talk about. What works in your life? What doesn't work? The gospel works, and it addresses what doesn't work.

It is the power of God for salvation to everyone who believes. Through the gospel, God forgives, heals, fills you with love and power, sets you free, and enables you to live an altogether different life. You know this if you believe the gospel, because if you believe it, you know how well it works. The gospel of Jesus Christ changes you. And when it changes you, you talk about it.

If we are going to be fluent in the gospel, we need to stop and reflect on how the gospel works in our lives. What has God done in you? How has he changed you? How is he at work in you right now? Maybe you currently need the power of the gospel at work in your life. What work do you need God to do in you today? How might the gospel work to address that? It's possible you haven't yet experienced God's power to save you. Or maybe it's been a while since you have walked in the power of the gospel to save you today. For this reason, I decided to place this section, "The Gospel in Me," before the next one, "The Gospel with Us." You won't be fluent in the gospel if the gospel isn't really good news to you yet.

We have a far greater story to tell than [any other story on earth]. We were enemies of God, hopeless and helpless, enslaved to sin and Satan, being crushed daily by his destructive blows. For hundreds of years, the world needed a Savior. We needed to be set free, forgiven, and restored. Jesus came, and it did not look good. He was from Nazareth, for goodness' sake! But he lived the life we couldn't. He went "undefeated" [by sin and death] for thirty-three years. Then, on the cross, it looked like it was over—and it was. But it wasn't a victory for evil. Jesus won as he rose again on the third day! Sin was paid for, Satan was crushed, and death was dealt a deathblow. Jesus made a public spectacle of Satan, sin, and death, and overcame for us.

Now we are free, forgiven, loved, and more than conquerors! Do you believe it? Do you love it? Do you love him? If so, tell the world! Tell your community. Tell your friends. Tell your spouse. Tell your children. Tell your neighbor. Tell your boss. Tell your coworkers. Tell your enemies. Tell them every day. Tell everyone that love has come to town and defeated death, hatred, sickness, and sorrow!

It's good news! It's great news! It's the gospel of Jesus Christ!

It starts in you and spills out of your heart through your mouth to the world, for it's out of the overflow of your heart that your mouth speaks. You will talk about him if you love him. If you don't, start talking about him, what's he's done, and what he's done for you, and you will love him. And you'll begin to see more and more clearly how wonderful his gospel is and how powerfully it works. As a result, you will talk about Jesus more and more.

Thoughtfully read the following passages of Scripture related to today's theme. Take a few moments to write down words and phrases that particularly struck you, as well as any thoughts or personal applications they prompted. Make these words a prayer to God.

Matthew 27:32–28:20

Luke 23:26–24:53

Romans 1:16–17

Ephesians 2:1–10

We Talk About What Works

To apply the concepts of this week's "Reading #2" in your everyday life, pray that God will open your eyes and guide you, then answer the following questions and complete the exercises.

1. "We like things to work. And when things work well, we talk about that. We also talk about what does not work for the same reason. Now, stop and think again about what you talk about. What works in your life? What doesn't work?"

2. Look back at the things you wrote down in answers to Powlison's "X-Ray" questions in Reflection #1. How many of your answers stem from believing that your answer produces or provides something for you, or otherwise somehow "works"?

3. The Bible says that God created the world, and that before sin, the world and everything in it was "good." Everything God created worshiped and glorified him; everything on earth saw God as the one who produces anything good, provides the earth with everything good. In other words, God was the ultimate "Worker" in his creation.

In previous weeks, we've seen this theme through a couple different lenses: In the Story of God, sin and brokenness are the ultimate, objective problems with the world—and the solution is Jesus. The "4 G Statements" (God is Good, Glorious, Great, and Gracious) are poignant because they remind us of truths in the midst of believing lies. In other words, "the gospel works, and it addresses what doesn't work." But if we're fully honest, at times it's just so hard to believe that the gospel is the solution to every problem and that God is the pinnacle of goodness, glory, greatness, and grace in our lives!

In chapter 9 of Mark's gospel, a distraught father of a demon-possessed boy asking Jesus to heal his son declares, "I believe; help my unbelief!" (v.24) In his head he knew Jesus was the answer, but in his heart he could not believe it. When you and I find ourselves in the same position, we'll be glad to know that Jesus did not unload the wrath of God on this man; instead, he not only healed the boy, but literally raised him from the dead!

This question may be difficult, but we'll ask you to be honest: prayerfully ask God to show you reasons you see other things as "working" better than him, and reasons you don't think he "works" in your life. Write down your answers.

4. Whether Question #3 was easy or difficult for you, prayerfully ask God to help you rightly consider the following. Write down a few thoughts for each:

   o What has God done in you? How has he changed you? How is he at work in you right now?

   o What work do you need God to do in you today? How might the gospel work to address that?

5. As you ponder the person and work of Jesus, and your love for him compared to your love of other things, read—and pray that God will help you believe and rest in—this truth: "You will talk about [Jesus] if you love him. If you don't, start talking about him, what's he's done, and what he's done for you, and you will love him. And you'll begin to see more and more clearly how wonderful his gospel is and how powerfully it works. As a result, you will talk about Jesus more and more. He is the best news there is." Consider writing out your thoughts and prayers as you reflect on this truth.

Capturing and Examining Our Thoughts

WEEK 3, READING 3

Thoughtfully read the following excerpts, or for more context and a deeper dive, read the first half of chapter 8 of *Gospel Fluency*, ending before the section titled "Bring the Thought into Submission."

We are at war! Bullets are flying. Bombs are dropping. The enemy is closing in. Destruction is all around. There are casualties everywhere. But in our war, you can't see any of this. Well, you can see the effects of it all over the place in the brokenness, chaos, and pain around us, but this war is invisible.

We are not fighting each other. Our war is not against "flesh and blood, but against the rulers, against the authorities, against the cosmic powers over this present darkness, against the spiritual forces of evil in the heavenly places" (Eph. 6:12). And we are not fighting with physical weapons. We fight what is unseen with weapons that are not wielded by human hands. Our battle is spiritual, and so are the weapons we use. The gospel is the power of God for salvation. And our enemies are the Devil, the world, and the flesh.

The Devil screams out: "God is evil.

I hate him and I will do everything to oppose him and destroy what he has made." The world screams out: "This world is best without God, and you are best when it's all about you." And the flesh screams out: "I don't need God because I am god. It's all about me and it's all dependent upon me."

So what are we to do in this battle? The Bible tells us to **1)** take our thoughts captive and examine them, **2)** bring them into submission, **3)** consider the fruit, and then **4)** fight with gospel truths. Week 4 gets into the second, third, and fourth steps; for now, we focus on the first.

What is going through your mind? What do you regularly hear spoken in your head? What are you believing about God, his work in Jesus, others, yourself, and what you should do? This is why it is so important to know the gospel, rehearse it in our minds, and remember it. We cannot defeat the enemies of our souls without becoming more gospel-fluent. And part of growing in gospel fluency is learning how to recognize what is not from God—what is not in line with the truths of the gospel.

So how do you know if what you're thinking lines up with what is true in the gospel? Well, remember that the gospel literally means "good news." So ask yourself: "Is this good news that I'm thinking? Is it tearing God down or lifting him up? Is it tearing others down or building them up? Is it tearing me down or encouraging, exhorting, or equipping me?" The enemy of our souls lies: Satan brings to our minds thoughts and words that are lies about God... One good way to learn how to discern the truth from a lie is to continue reading Scripture. If what you hear disagrees with the Bible, it's a lie.

Satan also accuses: he loves to tear us down with accusations. And most often he tries to deny what is true of us in Christ—what Jesus has done to change us. He doesn't want us to live boldly for Jesus, so he accuses us of things that are not true of us so that we will cower in fear, guilt, and shame . . . He also tempts us with promises of fulfillment through sinful pleasures or pursuits. He tries to convince us that God's ways are not good. And he loves to offer seductive short-cuts to fulfill our longings and desires. He often tries to make sin look attractive to lure our hearts away from obeying God . . . The enemy also loves to divide and isolate through gossip, slander, and bitterness.

The means vary, but our enemy loves to get us to turn against one another. He loves to erode our trust and give us reasons to separate or divide. And one of his greatest schemes is to isolate us as he does it. He wants us alone so he can pick us off one by one with no one around to encourage us or speak the truths of Jesus into our lives. Watch out for the schemes. In all of them, our enemy is dead set on our destruction.

The first step is to capture the thought and examine it. Train yourself to regularly stop and closely examine what you are thinking, feeling, or believing in light of the truths of the gospel.

Thoughtfully read the following passages of Scripture related to today's theme. Take a few moments to write down words and phrases that particularly struck you, as well as any thoughts or personal applications they prompted. Make these words a prayer to God.

2 Corinthians 11:12–14

Romans 8:1–11

Ephesians 6:10–20

1 Peter 5:8–11

1 John 2:15–17

Capturing and Examining Our Thoughts

WEEK 3, REFLECTION 3

To apply the concepts of this week's "Reading #3" in your everyday life, pray that God will open your eyes and guide you, then answer the following questions and complete the exercises.

1. Considering the content you read, define the three things that we're at war against.

2. In your own words, what does it mean to "take thoughts captive and examine them"?

3. The list below, from chapter 8 of *Gospel Fluency*, includes some of the common lies, accusations, temptations, and means of divisions and isolation that Satan puts in peoples' minds. Circle all those that you have believed at some point. Then put stars by the ones you find yourself still believing at times. In the spaces below, write some of those you've been working through up to this point in this *Handbook*.

Some of the *lies* you might hear are:

God doesn't really love you.

He's out to get you and destroy your life.

God has left you. You're all alone and he doesn't care. You're not that important to him.

Besides, even if he did love you, he couldn't help you. He's not that powerful.

He can't be everywhere, you know.

And even if he could, the stuff you're dealing with doesn't matter to him.

Satan also *accuses* through thoughts like:

You really blew it this time! You should be ashamed of yourself.

It shouldn't surprise you, however; you always do stuff like that. You're such a loser!

How many more times do you have to fail to realize it?

You're never going to amount to much of anything.

It's all because you're a filthy sinner. It's what you do. You're no saint, that's for sure.

He also *tempts* us with promises of fulfillment through sinful pleasures or pursuits, such as:

Look at this image—you know it will make you feel powerful or desired or aroused.

Go ahead, take one more drink. It will make all your trouble go away.

God knows this is enjoyable. He just doesn't want you to have any fun.

You deserve better. You've worked so hard, what's wrong with a little reward?

You know you need that. And if you get it, everything will change for you.

The enemy also loves to divide and isolate through gossip, slander, and bitterness:

Go ahead, say it. You know it's true.

Everyone else should know how much they've messed up as well.

Besides, think about how good it'll make you feel to be seen as better than them!

Put some spin on this one. Make the story a little juicier. People love scandal.

They really did hurt you! They deserve to suffer for that. Don't let it go.

They should pay. It's about time they got what was coming to them!

4. Look back at three or four of the phrases you starred or wrote in Question #3. Prayerfully ask yourself the following questions for each one, as you practice examining your thoughts. Write down answers that come to mind for some of these questions, for each phrase you consider.

    *   Is this really true? Or is it a lie?

    *   Is this from God or someone else?

    *   Does this sound like the Devil's accusation or the Spirit's conviction?

    *   Does it line up with the gospel of Jesus Christ?

    *   What am I hoping in right now? What do I believe this hope promises to give me?

- Why am I considering this behavior? What will be its outcome?

- In all of this, what is true of Jesus? What is true of who I am in him?

- How did Jesus do better for me? How did he speak a better word over me?

- What about Jesus do I need to remember and believe right now?

5. As you wrap up this week and ponder the truths of the gospel as a means of battling unbelief in God, read—and pray that God will help you believe and rest in—this truth: "Just as in learning a language, you need to capture and examine your thoughts to see if they line up with the gospel, then bring them into submission to Christ by regularly rehearsing the truths of the gospel to yourself over and over again. Remember, you don't have to do this alone. You have the Spirit of God with you to develop you in the gospel. Invite him to help you, to teach you, to bring to your mind all that is true of Jesus." Consider writing out your thoughts and prayers as you reflect on this truth.

Look Back

After completing your Readings and Reflections, and before your group meets this week, take a few moments to look over your readings and reflections: What have you learned? How has God shaped and impacted you? What do you especially want to remember, do, and/or share with your group this week?

Group Discussion

Looking back over this week's personal readings and reflection, discuss at least one or two of the following questions with a close community of friends. As you discuss, remember your commitment to be honest, and to help each other "grow up in Christ" by "speaking truth in love" with each other.

1. What concepts were new, or especially stood out, from this week's readings? What was difficult from the readings? What questions do you have from the readings?

2. As a group, how would we together describe the three things we battle, explain why the gospel is "good news," and define "love" (specifically as it relates to Jesus)?

Much of this week has been about the life of the mind: *my* belief and unbelief; sin, temptation, and accusation *I* believe; work of the flesh or fruit of the Spirit in *me*. And remember, this week only brought us to the halfway point of "The Gospel in Me." While next week will give you more practical ways to fight the war of our minds and to take our thoughts captive, use what you've already experienced—from this *Handbook* and otherwise—to practice helping increase each other's love and affection for Jesus.

3. Looking back over things you circled (not those you starred or wrote) in Reflection #3, share areas of unbelief that God has transformed into belief. Let this be a celebration with your friends, praising and thanking God for helping you know, love, and trust him more.

4. Look back at Reflection #1: What are some of the things you wrote down that you love and talk about more than Jesus? Discuss why those things are more exciting and appealing to you than Jesus. Ask each other to help you see Jesus as the object of your greatest affection, and to talk about him more.

5. Apply the gospel, even to this conversation: sometimes even admitting we need help—from God and others—is a difficult "first shot" in the war of the mind. Take a moment and discuss why it's difficult to admit our need for God and others, and why it's hard to ask others for help in our own fights for holiness. Consider those reasons, in light of this week's and previous weeks' content.

6. As we wrap up this week's difficult task of battling for truth, we acknowledge that it can be lonely—or impossible—if we try it alone. Are there any commitments your group needs to make to each other, as you pursue "regularly rehearsing the gospel" in each other's lives together?

Group Exercise

Stemming from this week's statements "we talk about what we love," "we love what we talk about," and "we love what works," walk through the following activity as a group. If your group is larger than about six people, you may want to divide into groups of three or four, to make sure everyone gets a chance to participate. This may be the most personal exercise to date, as you invite others to point out things in you that you may not see: be real, honest, prayerful, and loving, as you make these truths personal together.

First, have each person…

O Share a normal, everyday interaction you had this week, with someone in the group or otherwise. What did their words and actions show that they love? How did you know? What thoughts or emotions did that stir in you, toward that person? Any other thoughts? (If it's hard to talk about the conversation without falling into gossip, instead mention things you talked about, what it showed about yourself, etc.)

O Celebrate God's work in your own life, in helping you capture and examine new thoughts this week. What were some of the things he helped you see truth in, in Reflection #3, Question #4? Let this lead to a time of celebration for your group. God is helping you see truth in areas of unbelief!

After each person shares, together as a group...

O Encourage ways you've seen each person grow in gospel fluency, and celebrate specific ways you've seen their lives viewed more and more through the Story of God, and ways you've seen them grow in capturing and examining lies, accusations, and temptations.

O Celebrate God's work in each person. Specifically mention ways that each person's life and words point you toward Jesus, and ways you see God working in him/her and in your community.

✳ NOTE ✳

Enrich your learning and experience for this week by watching the companion video at **saturatetheworld.com/gf**

PRAY

Spend some time praying together, for your group and for each specific person: that God would help you see his story play out in everyday moments of your lives and that he will lead you to see it as the story that dominates your worldview; that he will keep Jesus' life, death, and resurrection consistently on your mind throughout each day; and that he increases your faith and draws you more and more toward belief in him, in all things.

The Gospel in Me

PART 2

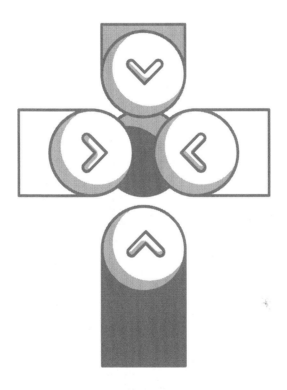

WEEK 4

This week is the second half of "The Gospel in Me." Last week's Readings and Reflections might have left you feeling a bit "low," as they were designed to help you define specific areas of need for the gospel. Like a good doctor, last week's goal was to examine the symptoms, define the problems, and bring us a diagnosis. This week's Readings and Reflections are designed to be "the cure for what ails you": as we continue fighting the war of the mind, Week 4 is a "remedy," helping apply the sweet truths of the gospel to the lies, accusations, and temptations we each defined last week.

Fighting for Truth

WEEK 4, READING 1

Thoughtfully read the following excerpts, or for more context and a deeper dive, read the second half of chapter 8 of *Gospel Fluency*, beginning with the section titled "Bring the Thought into Submission."

As we saw last week, we are always in the midst of a deep, spiritual battle. Every moment we [have] can be won or lost, as our thoughts are turned toward or against God and truth. Thus, the Bible tells us to 1) take our thoughts captive and examine them, 2) bring them into submission, 3) consider the fruit, and then 4) fight with gospel truths. Last week [we] considered

the first of these steps; today we turn toward the other three.

Once you've captured the thought, ask the Spirit to help you bring it into submission to Jesus. In other words, examine it enough to see if it lines up with what is true of God and his work in and through Jesus, and what is true of you as a result of your faith in Jesus. This is one of the reasons God sent his Spirit to us—to guide us into all truth, teach us what is true of Jesus, and regularly witness to us about these truths. He also convicts us of any unbelief in Jesus and reveals the lies we have believed (John 14-16).

When I first started to become aware of my need to grow in gospel fluency, this was not a natural process for me. I had to practice preaching the gospel to myself first. I regularly rehearsed the truths of the gospel at the beginning of my day:

- God is perfect. Jesus lived perfectly for me. He is my righteousness.

- God loves me. Jesus died for my sins. I am loved and forgiven.

- God is powerful and mighty. Jesus rose from the dead. I am more than a conqueror in him.

- God is alive and present and with me. He sent his Spirit to be with me and in me. I am not alone or without the power to overcome.

- God is for me and not against me.

Then, throughout my day, I had to preach the gospel to myself over and over again. I didn't do this alone. I asked the Holy Spirit to teach me, encourage me, remind me of what is true of Jesus, and convict and correct me when I was going the wrong way in my heart and mind.

If you are going to grow in gospel fluency, you need to do the same. Just as in learning a language, you need to capture and examine your thoughts to see if they line up with the gospel, then bring them into submission to Christ by regularly rehearsing the truths of the gospel to yourself over and over again.

One of the ways we fight the war of the mind is by considering the fruit we're experiencing or the fruit we would experience if we engaged a particular thought or suggested action. When I am not experiencing the fruit of the Spirit or my life is not resembling the life of Jesus, then clearly my mind is not set on the Spirit. That means my mind is not in submission to Christ. Whatever is in submission to Jesus Christ begins to look like Jesus and the fruit of the Spirit.

When I am teaching people how to fight with gospel truths, I introduce some cues to help them discover the aspect of the gospel they may need to press into. For instance, if someone is struggling with guilt or shame for what he has done, I encourage him to go to the cross where Jesus died and remember his words: "Father, forgive them, for they know not what they do" (Luke 23:34). We need the reminder that Jesus' death paid for all our sin, past, present, and future. He atoned for our sin, removed our guilt, and covered our shame.

If someone is struggling to overcome sin, I might encourage her to remember and believe in the resurrection, where Jesus condemned sin's power. He gives us the same power to overcome by the Spirit who raised him from the dead. Some are dealing with feelings of inadequacy in their behavior and lean toward performance-based acceptance. If so, I direct them to remember Jesus' life, perfectly lived in their place, and the Father's words spoken over Jesus (words that are now ours in Jesus): "This is my beloved Son, with whom I am well pleased" (Matt. 3:17).

Whatever the struggle, the life, death, burial, and resurrection of Jesus give life, hope, and power. By faith in Christ, every attribute, characteristic, and blessing that belongs to Jesus is available and accessible [to] us as we depend on and submit to him. We are co-heirs with Christ, blessed with every spiritual blessing in the heavenly realms, and he is present and ready to give us himself and anything we need to accomplish his will.

In essence, fighting with gospel truths is trusting in and putting on ourselves all that is true of Jesus, and therefore also true of us in Jesus. If you are going to become gospel fluent, you must be prepared to go to war. Take thoughts captive and examine them closely. Bring them into submission. Consider the fruit. Then fight with gospel truths.

Thoughtfully read the following passages of Scripture related to today's theme. Take a few moments to write down words and phrases that particularly struck you, as well as any thoughts or personal applications they prompted. Make these words a prayer to God.

John 14-16

Romans 12:1-2

Galatians 5:16-22

Colossians 3:1-4

Ephesians 6:10-20

Fighting for Truth

To apply the concepts of this week's "Reading #1" in your everyday life, pray that God will open your eyes and guide you, then answer the following questions and complete the exercises.

1. In your own words, what does it mean to "consider the fruit [of a particular thought or action]," and to "fight [lies, accusations, temptations, etc.] with gospel truths"?

2. Circling, starring, and/or writing phrases in Week 3, Reflection #3 is one way to "capture" and "examine" our thoughts, and battle lies, accusation, and temptation. You're paying attention to something untrue and are calling it out. Once you have done this, the next step in the battle is "submitting the thought": "ask[ing] the Spirit to help you bring it into submission to Jesus. In other words, examine it enough to see if it lines up with what is true of God and his work in and through Jesus, and what is true of you as a result of your faith in Jesus."

One at a time, look back at the phrases you starred or wrote in Week 3, Reflection #3. Under each statement, write an area of your life you feel it might need to be applied. In addition to the phrases already written, feel free to write a few other things you know to be true of God, that are particularly impacting as you submit your thoughts to Christ.

- O God is perfect. Jesus lived perfectly for me. He is my righteousness.

- O God loves me. Jesus died for my sins. I am loved and forgiven.

- O God is powerful and mighty. Jesus rose from the dead. I am more than a conqueror in him.

- O God is alive and present and with me. He sent his Spirit to be with me and in me. I am not alone or without the power to overcome.

- O God is for me and not against me.

- O

- O

- O

3. Without looking at the Bible, write down as many marks that Paul defines as the "work of the flesh" in Galatians 5, then as many marks that Paul defines as the "fruit of the Spirit." It's okay if you don't get them all. (Once you've written as many as you remember, read Galatians 5:16-23 and fill in the rest.)

Now look back at some of the phrases you starred or wrote in Week 3, Reflection #3, as still being areas of unbelief. Use the space below to write some of the lies, accusations, temptations, divisions, or isolations, and an area of your life you feel each might need to be applied—whether outwardly or even "secretly" (in your own heart and mind).

4. The Apostle Paul explains our weapon in the battle of our mind is the "armor of God" found in Ephesians 6:

> *Finally, be strong in the Lord and in the strength of his might. Put on the whole armor of God, that you may be able to stand against the schemes of the devil . . . Stand therefore, having fastened on the belt of truth, and having put on the breastplate of righteousness, and, as shoes for your feet, having put on the readiness given by the gospel of peace. In all circumstances take up the shield of faith, with which you can extinguish all the flaming darts of the evil one; and take the helmet of salvation, and the sword of the Spirit, which is the word of God, praying at all times in the Spirit.* (Eph 6:10-11, 14-18)

These "pieces of armor" are not things that we, mere humans, can pick up and wield by our own power. The truth of this passage is that Jesus alone is the fullness of each piece of the armor of God. On the next page, in the second column, write the ways that Jesus, through the gospel work, is the fulfillment of each phrase.

In the next column, write some specific ways that some of the armor above can especially help you battle the "work of the flesh" and produce "the fruit of the Spirit" in areas of unbelief.

Finally, write ways that seeing Jesus as the fullness of each piece of armor helps make us "strong in the Lord and in the strength of his might," as we "stand against the schemes of the devil" and let God fight for us in the war of our minds.

PIECES OF ARMOR	HOW IS JESUS THE FULFILLMENT?
THE BELT OF TRUTH	
THE BREASTPLATE OF RIGHTEOUSNESS	
THE SHOES OF READINESS GIVEN BY THE GOSPEL	
THE SHIELD OF FAITH	
THE HELMET OF SALVATION	
THE SWORD OF THE SPIRIT	
PRAYER IN THE SPIRIT	

HOW THE ARMOR HELPS YOU BATTLE AND PRODUCE FRUIT	HOW JESUS AS FULFILLMENT MAKES US STRONG AND ALLOWS GOD TO FIGHT FOR US

5. Pause to thank God that we don't go into war alone: God has created us to rely on his Spirit, and on each other, as we fight to love Jesus and as we battle sin, Satan, and our flesh. Read—and pray that God will help you believe and rest in—this truth: "Remember, you don't have to do this alone. You have the Spirit of God with you to develop you in the gospel. Invite him to help you, to teach you, to bring to your mind all that is true of Jesus. You should also be in community with others who know and love Jesus, who can help you in the battle." Consider writing out your thoughts and prayers as you reflect.

From Fruit to Root

WEEK 4, READING 2

Thoughtfully read the following excerpts, or for more context and a deeper dive, read the first half of chapter 9 of *Gospel Fluency*, stopping before the title "From Root to Fruit."

Part of our job in growing in gospel fluency is paying attention to the overflow of our hearts. What comes out in the form of thoughts, emotions, and behaviors finds its origin inside of us. Too often, we focus our attention on changing the external rather than addressing the internal. But Jesus was very clear that what defiles us proceeds from inside our hearts—our beliefs and our motives. The fruit of our lives comes from the roots of our faith. Just as a thermometer detects a fever, what we see or experience tells us about the gospel health of our hearts. So we need to learn to trace the fruit back to the root.

Over the years, I have learned to ask four key questions in progressive order when forming people in the gospel: **1)** Who is God? **2)** What has God done (which reveals who God is)? **3)** Who am I in light of God's work? and **4)** How should I live in light of who I am? I encourage people to apply these questions to their Bible study and to all of their discipleship processes.

When I am seeking to discern unbelief in the gospel, I reverse the order of those questions: **1)** What am I doing or experiencing right now? **2)** In light of what I am doing or experiencing, what do I believe about myself? **3)** What do I believe God is doing or has done? and **4)** What do I believe God is like? In other words, I trace the fruit back to the root. If the fruit is not like Jesus, that is an indicator that our faith is not in Jesus. Remember, we're all still unbelievers in many areas of our lives (as we saw in [Week] 1). We do not always believe the truths about God as revealed in the gospel; therefore, we are living in unbelief.

How do we know if the fruit of our lives is like Jesus? Well, it helps to get to know what Jesus is like. This is why we need to continue to become more and more acquainted with him by reading the Scriptures, especially the Gospels, which de-scribe how Jesus lived. The fruit of faith in Jesus is love for God and others. The gospel makes clear that this is not something we do on [our] own. Through faith in Jesus, each of us is made into a pure and holy dwelling place—a temple—where God's Spirit lives. Jesus foretold that he would send the Spirit to help us know, believe in, and be connected to Jesus so that we could bear much fruit.

[In *Gospel Fluency*], I shared how Tim Chester teaches that beneath every sin is a failure to believe a truth about God. I'm convinced the same applies to what we be-

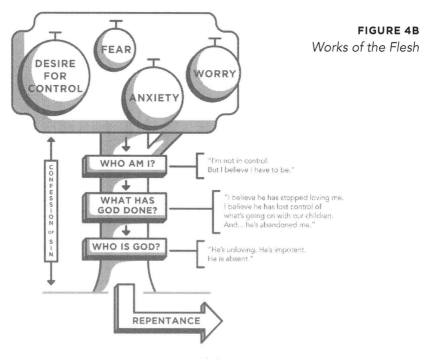

FIGURE 4B
Works of the Flesh

lieve about ourselves. Because we believe lies about God, we also believe lies about ourselves. We believe God is unloving, so we, in turn, believe we are unlovable—disposable, unwanted garbage. We believe God is not our Savior, so we have to be the savior to our friends, our spouses, or our children . . . We all fluctuate between the extremes of believing we are demigods sent to save the world and demons who are the scum of the earth, and everything in between. And the reason we believe what we do about ourselves is because of what we believe or don't believe about God.

We need to learn to speak our beliefs out loud. So often, we are not even aware of what we are believing in any given moment. We just go along, living in false belief, and, as a result, we continue to engage in sinful behaviors. I am so blessed to have a friend and partner in Jayne who encourages me to speak out loud what is going on in my heart between me and God. She is in good company with the psalmists and the prophets in the Scriptures. They knew that our transformation comes partly through our verbal proclamation of our faith—speaking out loud what we are believing in the moment. This is confession.

So often, when people are led to confess their sins, they only confess their sinful behaviors. In other words, they confess the fruit. They say: "I'm sorry I lied. Please forgive me." Or: "I looked at pornography. I know that's wrong. Please forgive me." The problem, however, is that they need to confess their sinful beliefs—the roots, the stuff below the surface that is motivating and producing their behaviors, the sin beneath the sins. All sin stems from wrong beliefs—lies we believe—and ultimately from our unbelief in Jesus. And because we generally don't go beyond the fruit to the root, we end up aiming at behavior modification instead of gospel transformation. In the gospel, we come to see that sin is wicked and our world is broken. People suffer and will suffer because of sin. We are not promised a pain-free, trouble-free, suffering-free existence. But we don't need more self-help and we don't need denial. We need deliverance.

When we address only the behaviors and push people to change what they do without a change in what they believe, the weight falls on us rather than God to handle the problems of the world and deal with the brokenness caused by sin. Instead, we need to trust in God's power to change us and change the world. [We need] gospel transformation, not just behavior modification. God's Spirit is our guide, teacher, and counselor. When those of us who belong to God confess out loud what we believe, the Spirit is right there with us to convict us of our unbelief and lead us to the truth that is in Jesus. This is how God grants us repentance. He convicts us of our unbelief and leads us to believe the truth.

Thoughtfully read the following passages of Scripture related to today's theme. Take a few moments to write down words and phrases that particularly struck you, as well as any thoughts or personal applications they prompted. Make these words a prayer to God.

Matthew 22:34-40

John 14:1-14

Galatians 5:19-23

From Fruit to Root

WEEK 4, REFLECTION 2

To apply the concepts of this week's "Reading #2" in your everyday life, pray that God will open your eyes and guide you, then answer the following questions and complete the exercises.

1. Considering the content you read, in your own words define "confession."

2. Take a few moments of personal worship and write down as many answers as you can to each of the following questions:

   O Who is God (what are some things he reveals as his identity, especially toward his people)?

   O What has God done (in general, and especially through the person and work of Jesus)?

   O Who am I in light of God's work (what things does God declare to be true about our own identity)?

   O How should I live in light of who I am (how should answers to the other questions impact how we think or live)?

3. "When I am seeking to discern unbelief in the gospel, I reverse the order of those questions: **1)** What am I doing or experiencing right now? **2)** In light of what I am doing or experiencing, what do I believe about myself? **3)** What do I believe God is doing or has done? and **4)** What do I believe God is like? In other words, I trace the fruit back to the root. If the fruit is not like Jesus, that is an indicator that our faith is not in Jesus."

Area of Unbelief or Struggle *Write area here* ——————▶	
What am I doing or experiencing right now?	
In light of what I am doing or experiencing, what do I believe about myself?	
What do I believe God is doing or has done?	
What do I believe God is like?	

Look back at the first three weeks of this *Handbook*. Consider as many areas of unbelief (Week 1), lesser stories (Week 2), and lies, accusations, and temptations (Week 3) you've identified so far. For the rest of this Reflection, practice the "fruit to root" process by walking through as many of those areas as possible using the following questions. Be honest: and it's okay if you can't fully answer every question for every area of unbelief you try; you'll have an opportunity to ask your close community for help at this week's meeting.

4. As you consider the root disbelief in each area above, turn your answers into prayers of confession to God. Ask his forgiveness not just for your behaviors, but for the beliefs—or unbeliefs—that lie at the root of each.

5. Now that we've deconstructed areas of unbelief, Reading and Reflection #3 reconstructs us with a right belief in God, based on the gospel of Jesus through the power of the Spirit. Read—and pray that God will help you believe and rest in—this truth: "God's Spirit is our guide, teacher, and counselor. When those of us who belong to God confess out loud what we believe, the Spirit is right there with us to convict us of our unbelief and lead us to the truth that is in Jesus. This is how God grants us repentance. He convicts us of our unbelief and leads us to believe the truth." Consider writing out your thoughts and prayers as you reflect.

From Root to Fruit

WEEK 4, READING 3

Thoughtfully read the following excerpts, or for more context and a deeper dive, read the second half of chapter 9 of *Gospel Fluency*, beginning at the section titled "From Root to Fruit."

In Reading #2, we saw Jeff's four key questions to ask in progressive order when forming people in the gospel: **1)** Who is God? **2)** What has God done (which reveals who God is)? **3)** Who am I in light of God's work? and **4)** How should I live in light of who I am? I encourage people to apply these questions to their Bible study and to all of their discipleship processes. I do this because we all do what we do because of what we believe about **1)** who God is, **2)** what God has done, and **3)** who we are in Christ or apart from Christ. The roots of our faith produce the fruit of our life.

Reading and Reflection #2 asked those questions in reverse order, as an exercise that worked from outside in. But once we've discovered the root issue—the specific areas of unbelief—we're only halfway done. Once we've deconstructed falsehood and unbelief, we now rebuild our faith with truth and right belief. In other words, once we've gone from "Fruit to Root," we turn and go from "Root to Fruit.": First we ask, "What do you believe about God? Who is God?" It may be helpful to write answers to this and forthcoming questions on the side of the tree trunk, starting at the bottom and moving up with each question (see Figure 4A on the next page).

Once we answer the first question, we ask the second: "[H]ow do we know #1 is true? What has God done, that shows us who he is?") Before we move on, it is important to note how important this second question is. So often, when a Christian tries to encourage another person to believe or behave differently, he fails to proclaim the gospel—the good news about what God has done in Jesus Christ to reveal himself to us and to change us.

So we ask this second question, and praise God for the tangible ways he shows us—in our lives, in the Bible, and throughout history—his truth. It may help to ask and answer these first two questions multiple times, as we declare different truths about God, and remember and celebrate ways he's proven those things: "[W]hat else do you believe about God? . . . How do you know that? What has he done to show us this is true?" As we continue to speak out loud the truths God reveal[ed] to us through the gospel, [we experience] a change. [We are] transformed by the renewal of [our] mind, just as Paul says in

FIGURE 4A
Fruit of the Spirit

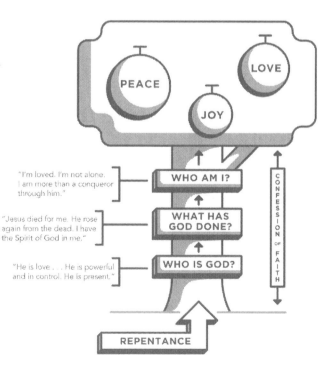

Romans 12:2. This wasn't just behavior modification. This [is] much deeper. This [is] gospel transformation, which always leads to behavioral change.

By now our answers are working their way up the trunk of the tree, to the fruit produced by our newly-rooted right belief. So we ask the final two questions, over and over, and we celebrate God's work in the answers he brings to mind by his Spirit. "What are you believing about yourself now? Who are you in light of God's work?" And "What are you experiencing? How should I live as a response to this?" We are not saved just once in our past. We continue being saved in the present. God's salvation didn't just happen to us. It is also continuing to happen. He is actively saving us. The gospel is good news for our sanctification—the ongoing work of God saving us and conforming us daily into the image of Christ. Our activity in this process is ongoing repentance from unbelief to belief in the gospel.

Since Readings #2 and #3 work together, I encourage you to begin paying close attention to the fruit of your life, but don't make the mistake of engaging in a self-change project. With the help of the Spirit, and ideally in community with others who love Jesus and believe the gospel, practice tracing the fruit to the root. Examine what you have been believing and where your beliefs are not in line with the truth of the gospel. Confess what you believe out loud. What is the sin under the sins? What sinful beliefs have you been holding?

Once you trace the fruit to the root, invite the Spirit to reveal the truth of who God is and what he has done for you in Christ. Ask him to give you the ability to see and believe the truth, repent from lies or unbelief, and turn to God in faith through Jesus. In other words, work your way from root to fruit. This will require knowing the gospel and spending regular time reading the Bible so as to be more equipped to speak the truth of God to the circumstances or situations you find yourself or others in.

If you begin to do this more often, you will find yourself being transformed more and more into the image of Jesus Christ. As a result, you will also become more and more fluent in the gospel, because the more you are changed by the gospel, the more you will want to talk about it. We all talk about what most affects us. And as you do, you and others will become more fluent together.

Thoughtfully read the following passages of Scripture related to today's theme. Take a few moments to write down words and phrases that particularly struck you, as well as any thoughts or personal applications they prompted. Make these words a prayer to God.

2 Corinthians 3:4-18 *(and you might look back at Galatians 5:19-23 again)*

From Root to Fruit

WEEK 4, REFLECTION 3

To apply the concepts of this week's "Reading #3" in your everyday life, pray that God will open your eyes and guide you, then answer the following questions and complete the exercises.

1. Considering the content you read, in your own words define "repentance."

2. Deconstructing specific areas of unbelief is only half the process. For this exercise, we reconstruct a right belief of God as it relates to those specific areas of unbelief.

   Paul said that as we repent and believe the gospel—as we turn to, look at, and believe in Jesus—we are transformed, increasingly becoming more and more like Jesus:

   > *"And we all, with unveiled face, beholding the glory of the Lord, are being transformed into the same image from one degree of glory to another. For this comes from the Lord who is the Spirit"* (2 Cor. 3:18).

Pick a few of the areas of unbelief you deconstructed in Reflection #2. Then spend the rest of today's reflection answering the following questions as they relate to each specific area of unbelief.

Area of Unbelief or Struggle *Write area here* ⟶	
Who is God? List as many things as you can about God's identity that specifically relate to this area of struggle/disbelief. (Ex. "God is love" or "just" or "our Father")	
What has God done? How has God proven each answer to the previous question in his work in the world and especially through the person and work of Jesus?	
Who am I in light of God's work? List as many true statements about who you are that you can think of.	
How should I live in light of who I am? What beliefs are you experiencing in light of the first three questions? How do you see them changing you?	

3. As you wrap up this week and ponder the truths of the gospel as a means of battling unbelief in God, read—and pray that God will help you believe and rest in—this truth: "Once you trace the fruit to the root, invite the Spirit to reveal the truth of who God is and what he has done for you in Christ. Ask him to give you the ability to see and believe the truth, repent from lies or unbelief, and turn to God in faith through Jesus. In other words, work your way from root to fruit. This will require knowing the gospel and spending regular time reading the Bible so as to be more equipped to speak the truth of God to the circumstances or situations you find yourself or others in." Consider writing out your thoughts and prayers as you reflect.

Look Back

After completing your Readings and Reflections, and before your group meets this week, take a few moments to look over your readings and reflections. What have you learned? How has God shaped and impacted you? What do you especially want to remember, do, and/or share with your group this week?

Group Discussion

Looking back over this week's personal readings and reflection, discuss at least one or two of the following questions with a close community of friends. As you discuss, remember your commitment to be honest and to help each other "grow up in Christ" by "speaking truth in love" with each other.

1. What concepts were new, or especially stood out from this week's readings? What was difficult from the readings? What questions do you have from the readings?

2. As a group, how would we together describe "submitting our thoughts," and define "confession" and "repentance"?

This week's theme has centered around the methodical deconstruction of disbelief and reconstructing a right worldview of belief in God, as it relates to specific areas we wrestle with. It's the second week we consider the gospel in ourselves, and it's a vital piece of becoming fluent in the gospel.

3. Look back at Reflection #1: In what ways are the fruit of the Spirit (Gal. 5) and the armor of God (Eph. 6) only possible if we see our lives through a gospel lens? Why is it difficult to adopt such a lens?

4. Considering Reflections #2 and #3, why is it so easy to miss the "root" of our sin and disbelief, and instead try to merely solve or fix the "fruit"? What's the result, both short-term and long-term of stopping at the "fruit" instead of getting to the "root"?

5. Apply the gospel, even to this conversation: sometimes it's hard to get to the root of things. Discuss why it's difficult to "dig beneath the surface," and why it's hard to ask others for help in our own fights for holiness. Consider those reasons, in light of this week's and previous weeks' content.

6. Next week turns to consider "the gospel with us"—our need for each other as we grow in gospel fluency. As you consider that, are there any commitments your group needs to make to each other, as you pursue "regularly rehearsing the gospel" in each other's lives together?

Group Exercise

While the war of the mind is a personal war for everyone, it doesn't have to be an individual war. It's helpful to know that the ultimate Helper—God the Spirit—and those in your close community are in the foxhole with you, fighting on the front lines for your holiness. In chapter 8 of *Gospel Fluency*, Jeff writes:

When I am teaching people how to fight with gospel truths, I introduce some cues to help them discover the aspect of the gospel they may need to press into. For instance, if someone is struggling with guilt or shame for what he has done, I encourage him to go to the cross where Jesus died and remember his words: "Father, forgive them, for they know not what they do" (Luke 23:34). We need the reminder that Jesus' death paid for all our sin, past, present, and future. He atoned for our sin, removed our guilt, and covered our shame.

If someone is struggling to overcome sin, I might encourage her to remember and believe in the resurrection, where Jesus condemned sin's power. He gives us the same power to overcome by the Spirit who raised him from the dead.

Some are dealing with feelings of inadequacy in their behavior and lean toward performance-based acceptance. If so, I direct them to remember Jesus's life, perfectly lived in their place, and the Father's words spoken over Jesus (words that are now ours in Jesus): "This is my beloved Son, with whom I am well pleased" (Matt. 3:17).

Whatever the struggle, the life, death, burial, and resurrection of Jesus give life, hope, and power. And by faith in Christ, every attribute, characteristic, and blessing that belongs to Jesus is available to us because of our unity with him.

In essence, fighting with gospel truths is trusting in and putting on ourselves all that is true of Jesus, and therefore also true of us in Jesus.

This week's group exercise puts that into practice, as you consider going from "fruit to root" then from "root to fruit" together. If your group is larger than about six people, you may want to divide into groups of three or four to make sure everyone gets a chance to participate. We'll encourage you to "let your group in"—especially if there are areas where you're having a hard time reconstructing right belief. It may be hard to be this transparent and vulnerable, but by God's design you need each other in those areas especially!

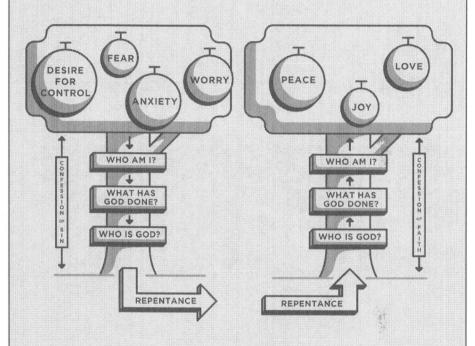

First, looking at the Tree Diagrams and considering the four questions, have each person ...

O   ... share one or two areas of unbelief they processed in Reflection #2 and #3 and specific ways that God used that process to establish greater belief in their hearts and minds

o   … share at least one area that they need help deconstructing disbelief based on the "fruit to root" process, and reconstructing right belief based on the "root to fruit" process.

After each person shares, together as a group…

o   … celebrate God's work in each person as he worked through his Spirit to establish new areas of belief in former unbelief.

o   … lovingly serve each other as you help deconstruct unbelief and re-construct right belief in areas they need help.

o   … consider if there are any commitments you need to make to help each other live consistently in light of newfound belief.

> *** N O T E ***
>
> 1. Next week's group exercise is sharing a meal together, and we'll encourage you to go a little "above and beyond" for that meal. Before you end tonight's group meeting, make a plan: What will you eat? Who will bring what? Will you prepare food beforehand or will you make it together? Plan well today to get the full experience of next week's exercise!
>
> 2. Enrich your learning and experience for this week by watching the companion video at **saturatetheworld.com/gf**

PRAY

Spend some time praying together, for your group and for each specific person: that God would produce increasing fruit of the Spirit in each of you; that he would give you the strength—and namely his own power—as you fight the battle for your mind; and that he would grow each person's ability and ease in deconstructing disbelief and reconstructing right belief.

The Gospel With Us

PART 1

WEEK 5

This week is the first half of considering "The Gospel with Us." While God works in individual people, his history-long aim is to recreate for himself a people. So while the gospel applies to us personally, it also applies to us corporately. This week's Readings and Reflections give the first three of seven specific practices, designed to help draw your community more strongly together, as you specifically consider the familial nature of our life in Christ.

Eating to Remember

WEEK 5, READING 1

Thoughtfully read the following excerpts, or for more context and a deeper dive, read the first half of chapter 10 of *Gospel Fluency*, ending before the section titled "The Meal."

If you and others around you are going to grow in gospel fluency, you need consistent immersion in a gospel-speaking community. This needs to be much more than a weekly gathering of the church where the gospel is preached (though it should include this). It also should be more than a weekly Bible study, small-group gathering, or missional-community meeting (though I also recommend these). Growth in gospel fluency requires regularly being with others who know and love Jesus, speak about him often, and commit together to regularly remind one another of the gospel when they forget.

From the very beginning of the story, the act of eating has played a very significant role in the worship and remembrance of who God is, what he has done, and who we are. God provided a great place for Adam and Eve to live, with all the food they needed. They regularly had the opportunity to remember God, his word, and his work, as well as who they were and what they were called to do. For them, every meal was a time to remember God's abundant provision and express their worship of him alone.

When we eat, we see that our food looks good. Some meals look like a painting by Monet, others look like a Picasso, but they are all works of art. We can smell our food. Just think of all the wonderful aromas of the best meals you've had. Don't you love them! And as you put your food in your mouth, there's an explosion of sensations—sweet, sour, bitter, salty. It's like a party in your mouth! And you don't just taste your food, you feel it as well. There are so many textures to experience. And then you hear it as it crunches, or sloshes or slurps its way into your body (some people are annoyed at this part of eating). Through all of this, you are nourished and replenished, strengthened and rebuilt. God wants us to eat and remember—enjoy and worship him—and, at the same time, have our needs met by him.

Remember what he said to Adam and Eve: "Eat from any tree in the garden except the tree of the knowledge of good and evil. If you eat of that tree, you will surely die" (see Gen. 2:16–17). Every meal was an opportunity to remember, trust, and obey. Every meal was meant to be an act of remembrance and worship. But they didn't remember, trust, and obey. They ate unto themselves. God designed them to trust in his ability to provide for them. Something outside of them was meant to take care of a deep need inside of them—and he would provide that something. They were not to look outside of his provision.

All of this was meant to point us toward God's ultimate provision in Jesus. Eventually, Jesus came to be God's ultimate provision for us. He is the bread of life that meets our deepest needs and satisfies our greatest longings. Every meal is meant to cause us to remember and worship Jesus.

What if you took time at every meal—even very simple ones—to give thanks to God, praying not just at the beginning, but throughout the meal? Our family is trying to use our evening mealtimes more intentionally. We are presently rehearsing the Ten Commandments and going through the gospel with each one of them. We also have given each night a theme to guide what we do together at the meal—this is further described in Reflection #1.

There is one meal specifically given by Jesus, to remember and proclaim the gospel—we'll see that later this week. But for now, consider our normal, everyday meals: What if your friends, your family, your small group, or your missional community made it a point to make every single meal a remembrance and worship experience? What if you slowed down enough to remember Jesus at every meal? What if you savored every moment as an opportunity to praise God?

Thoughtfully read the following passages of Scripture related to today's theme. Take a few moments to write down words and phrases that particularly struck you, as well as any thoughts or personal applications they prompted. Make these words a prayer to God.

Genesis 1-3

Isaiah 25:6-12

Luke 7:33-35

Luke 19:1-10

Philippians 2:1-11

Revelation 19:6-10

Eating to Remember

WEEK 5, REFLECTION 1

One way your community can begin to regularly rehearse the gospel together is in the everyday meals you eat together each week. To apply the concepts of this week's "Reading #1" in your everyday life, pray that God will open your eyes and guide you, then answer the following questions and complete the exercises.

1. Considering the content you read, in your own words describe some of the ways that meals can remind us of who God is and what he's done.

2. How has God designed meals to be pictures of both necessary provision and multi-sensory joy? Which of those realities do you most easily lean toward as you consider food? Why? What's the danger in seeing food merely as provision or merely as joy-giving?

3. In 1 Corinthians 10:31, the apostle Paul charges followers of Jesus, "whether you eat or drink, or whatever you do, do all to the glory of God." How can the act of eating remind us of our need for Jesus, and how can it lead us to worship God?

4. In chapter 10 of *Gospel Fluency*, Jeff describes his family's weekly rhythms of intentionality with meals: On Mission Monday, we remember together our family's mission to glorify God and fulfill his purposes in saving us… Teaching Tuesday is when one of the children takes responsibility for our learning from God's word at the meal… With-Family Wednesday is the night we eat with our missional community… Thanksgiving Thursday is when we take time to give thanks for all God has done… On Fun Friday, we go out to eat, or we eat together and then go to a movie, have a game night, or take a special outing… Serving Saturday often means we are with others for a meal or serving some people… And Sunday is when we remember Jesus through taking communion together at our church's gathering (to be considered further in Reading and Reflection #2; for more on this weekly rhythm, see *Gospel Fluency*, chapter 10).

What are some ways that you and your family and/or friends can view meals with greater intentionality? With what people should you eat regularly, how often, and why? What could that look like, and when will you start?

5. As you consider celebrating God through eating normal, everyday meals with others, read—and pray that God will help you believe and rest in—this truth: "Jesus came to be God's ultimate provision for us. He is the bread of life that meets our deepest needs and satisfies our greatest longings. Every meal is meant to cause us to remember and worship Jesus." Consider writing out your thoughts and prayers as you reflect.

The Meal

WEEK 5, READING 2

Thoughtfully read the following excerpts, or for more context and a deeper dive, read the second half of chapter 10 of *Gospel Fluency*, beginning with the section titled "The Meal."

On the night Jesus was betrayed, he shared the Passover meal with his disciples. That meal commemorated the night when God struck down every firstborn son of Egypt while protecting his people from the same fate. Their protection came through the Passover lambs that were sacrificed and eaten inside homes where the doorposts had been covered with the lambs' blood. This was the final straw for Pharaoh, and he finally let God's people go. Ever after, the Passover was a remembrance meal of God's redemption of Israel out of slavery.

At his last meal with his disciples before his death, Jesus showed how every Passover meal was point-ing to him. And at this meal, Jesus changed the Passover to the Lord's Supper as his meal. It became a meal at which we remember how he redeemed us out of slavery to sin and Satan by becoming the true and better sacrificial Lamb of God for us.

Jesus picked up the bread, and when he had given thanks, he broke it and gave it to them, say-ing: "This is my body, which is given for you. Do this in remembrance of me." And he took a cup, and when he had given thanks, he gave it to them, and they all drank of it. And he said to them, "This is my blood of the covenant, which is poured out for many." Paul said,

"For as often as you eat this bread and drink the cup, you proclaim the Lord's death until he comes" (1 Cor. 11:26). We should remember him regularly with the meal and practice proclaiming his death to each other through it.

Another helpful practice for both remembrance and growth in gospel proclamation is to speak the gospel through the elements to each other's needs, hurts, and longings in small-group gatherings or missional-community meetings. I first tried this during a missional-community gathering at our home in January several years back. I explained to our group that I wanted each of them to share something they were struggling with; a desire they had that was yet to be met; or doubts or fears they might be experiencing. Then one of us would take the bread and the cup, and speak the truths of Jesus' body given and blood shed for us to the need... We [went] around the circle: one after another, we confessed our need for a Savior, and one after another, we proclaimed the good news of Jesus to our very real needs. It was an incredibly joyous and tear-filled experience of grace!

I've led this same experience many times now with brand-new Christians as well as church leaders. It isn't always the same experience. Some are not very fluent in the gospel and therefore struggle with how to speak it to specific needs. However, I let people know that's okay when I start and that those in the group will help one another. I usually ask for someone to volunteer to share, and let the person to the right know he or she will be asked to speak the gospel to the need. I then say: "If you don't know what to say, let us know and the rest of us will help. Over time, we will all get better at this."

God has given us many ways to remember him and grow in proclaiming the gospel. They are around us all the time in what is called general revelation—creation and the rhythms of life within it. Our job is to learn to see the truths of God around us and speak the truths of the gospel into it. The meal—"the Jesus Supper"—is the one he told us to use to regularly remember him. It is also one of the most effective ways I have found to train us to do this in all the other places of life as well.

Start with the [M]eal [communion] every week, then practice remembering Jesus at [other] meals, and you will have twenty-two stops through your week in gospel remembrance and proclamation. If you do this, you will be well on your way to growing in gospel fluency with others!

Thoughtfully read the following passages of Scripture related to today's theme. Take a few moments to write down words and phrases that particularly struck you, as well as any thoughts or personal applications they prompted. Make these words a prayer to God.

*Read at least one Gospel account of Jesus' Last Supper.

*Matthew 26:17-29

*Mark 14:12-25

*Luke 22:7-23

1 Corinthians 11:17-33

The Meal

WEEK 5, REFLECTION 2

A second way your community can regularly rehearse the gospel together is by participating together in the Lord's Supper with intentionality. To apply the concepts of this week's "Reading #2" in your everyday life, pray that God will open your eyes and guide you, then answer the following questions and complete the exercises.

1. Considering the content you read, in your own words describe the concept of "the Lord's Supper" or "communion" (or in some traditions, "eucharist").

2. What has been your understanding of and personal experience with "the Lord's Supper"? If there is brokenness, misunderstanding, or even guilt or baggage associated with this, are there ways the gospel can become good news, even to that reality? In what ways can others help you through that?

3. In what ways can you see it as remembering Jesus' death for our sins? In what ways can you see it as a proclamation of that death, to ourselves and to others?

4. In chapter 10 of *Gospel Fluency*, Jeff describes how the Lord's Supper, taken in community, can be a meaningful venue for speaking good news over each other: "[A] helpful practice for both remembrance and growth in gospel proclamation is to speak the gospel through the elements to each other's needs, hurts, and longings in small-group gatherings or missional-community meetings."

    While you'll have the opportunity to carry this out with your group at this week's meeting, consider this personally now: in what specific ways is Jesus' death, which we remember and proclaim with the bread and wine of communion, good news to the areas you've been wrestling through over the course of this *Handbook*? Spend a decent amount of time on this question, answer it in light of the different areas of struggle, and worship God for Jesus' death for every one of those struggles.

5. As you wrap up this focus on the specific meal by which Jesus calls his followers to remember him, read—and pray that God will help you believe and rest in—this truth: "God has given us many ways to remember him and grow in proclaiming the gospel. They are around us all the time in what is called general revelation—creation and the rhythms of life within it. Our job is to learn to see the truths of God around us and speak the truths of the gospel into it." Consider writing out your thoughts and prayers as you reflect.

He's the Better...

WEEK 5, READING 3

Thoughtfully read the following excerpts, or for more context and a deeper dive, read the first half of chapter 11 of *Gospel Fluency*, ending before the section titled "Get to Know the Overall Story."

"I can't stand my job! I've been working there for too long to be treated like this," she said.

We had just started eating dinner at our weekly missional community family meal when one of our members started unloading her frustrations about work. "I should have received a raise a long time ago and I am still in the same position that I started in two years ago," she went on to say. "My boss keeps telling me I will eventually get a promotion, but it seems like I keep getting overlooked. I'm really tired of this! I'm ready to quit." She continued sharing her frustrations about the working conditions and the poor benefits, and how her co-

workers didn't help the situation, as most of them had bad attitudes and poor work ethics.

This is a pretty normal occurrence for group life in a church— and for life in community anywhere, for that matter. We struggle with work and want a place to vent. Likewise, we experience pain and frustration in our relationships. Roommates get on our nerves. Finances are not always abundant or predictable. Parents wound us or let us down. So do our children. We have plenty to talk about and often much to complain about.

Typically, in a gathering like this, the initial response to our sister's complaints is often additional complaining: "I know what you mean! My job stinks as well." "You deserve better! Your boss doesn't know what he has in you. Maybe one day he'll wake us and realize what an incredible person you are!" "Yeah, well, it might be too late when he does, because if I were you, I'd quit!" A gospel community can do better than that.

I regularly encourage our groups to ask these questions: **1)** How does the gospel bring good news to this situation? **2)** What about the gospel do we need to hear right now? **3)** What about the gospel have we forgotten or failed to believe? and **4)** How is Jesus better than what we have or what we want?

Part of our job as a gospel-fluent community is to continue to remind one another that Jesus is "the Better." He is the better boss. He is also the better worker, who did a far better job than us. He is the better friend. He is the better Son, who perfectly obeyed the Father on our behalf—and on our children's behalf as well.

Parents, some of you need to remember this. Your children fail.

They're not perfect. And they were not meant to live the life you thought you should have. Many parents are trying to live vicariously through their children, silently saying to them: "Be the athlete I wish I had been. Get the grades I could never earn. Gain the popularity I could never attain. Give me the relationship I never had with my parents."

So many parents see their children as substitutes for their childhood. But children can't handle this weight. It will crush them. And that will disappoint parents who think this way. There is only one perfect child. Jesus is the better child. Your children need to know and believe this. You do as well. Maybe you're not the parent. Maybe you're the child who needs to know that Jesus is better. Jesus shows us the better Father and is for us the better Son.

This is what we need to practice doing together in our groups. We need to keep pointing each other to Jesus and showing how he is the Better everything. How do we do this? First, as a reminder, it is important to establish the group in the four key questions that we walked through in Week 4: **1)** Who is God/Jesus? **2)** What has he done or what is he doing? **3)** Who are we in light of that work? and **4)** How should we live in light of who we are?

Let's think about how these questions might have been answered in regard to [a] young woman with an unlikeable job and bad boss. **1)** Who is God/Jesus? Jesus is her Lord, her boss. And he is a good, great, gracious, and generous boss! **2)** What has he done for her (in other words, how do we know he is a good boss)? He did not come to be served but to serve and give his life as her ransom. He didn't give her the wages she deserves. The wages of sin is death, but the gift of God is eternal life through Jesus Christ our Lord (the better boss). And he sat down at the right hand of God the Father, where he is making constant intercession (speaking great words on her behalf) with the Father for her. **3)** Who is she in light of that work? She is seated with him in the heavenly realms, a child of God, approved of by the Father, a beneficiary of all that belongs to Jesus, and she now serves as an ambassador for the King of kings. **4)** How should she live? She should work with joy, freedom, power, and hope.

We go to work for Jesus, the only boss worthy of our worship, deserving of our thanks, and capable of granting us genuine, lasting approval. In Reflection #3 we'll try the same exercise with any situation or struggle. As a matter of practice, pick a relationship or situation (spouse, friend, child, work, provision, identity) and work through these questions together as a group.

Thoughtfully read the following passages of Scripture related to today's theme. Take a few moments to write down words and phrases that particularly struck you, as well as any thoughts or personal applications they prompted. Make these words a prayer to God.

Consider God's "better" role in the relationships described in 1 Timothy 5:1-6:3 and Colossians 3:18-4:1.

Ephesians 4:1-7

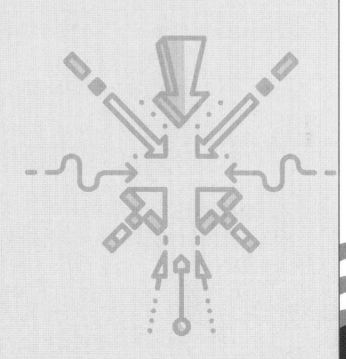

He's the Better...

This week's final way for your community to rehearse the gospel together is by helping each other see Jesus as "the Better," compared to everything and everyone else in your lives. To apply the concepts of this week's "Reading #3" in your everyday life, pray that God will open your eyes and guide you, then answer the following questions and complete the exercises.

1. Considering the content you read, in your own words describe as many benefits as you can of living alongside a close community of people who know Jesus and can press you toward the gospel.

2. Part of our job as a gospel-fluent community is to continue to remind one another that Jesus is "the Better." He is the better boss. He is also the better worker, who did a far better job than us. He is the better friend. He is the better Son, who perfectly obeyed the Father on our behalf—and on our children's behalf as well. How has your community served you well over the past several weeks and helped you on your journey into gospel fluency? Is there anyone you need to express gratitude to, who has helped you in specific ways?

3. We can be honest and consider the other side of question #1 as well: list as many difficulties as you can think of, of living alongside a close community of people who know Jesus and can press you toward the gospel. Why are those things hard? This week reminds us of the four questions (Who is God? What has he done? Who are we? How should we live?)—how might we need to ask those four questions related to the difficulties of living in community?

4. The first column on the next page lists various relationships that many people exist in. Regardless of how "good" or "bad" each human relationship is for you, the reality of Reading #3 is that Jesus is "the Better" version of that relationship: he fulfills the idealized version of it; he will never let us down as other humans do. In his life, death, and resurrection, Jesus proves himself "better." Use the chart on the next page for at least three relationships. Write a few words in the first column describing the human version of your experience. In the second column write a few words that describe Jesus, as he fulfills that role and relationship in an objectively greater way. (Feel free to add other relationships.)

5. As you rest in the fact that Jesus is the Better everything and everyone, read—and pray that God will help you believe and rest in—this truth: "This is what we need to practice doing together in our groups. We need to keep pointing each other to Jesus and showing how he is the Better everything." Consider writing out your thoughts and prayers as you reflect.

ROLES	HUMAN IN THAT ROLE	JESUS IN THAT ROLE
Spouse		
Sibling		
Best Friend		
Boss		
Child		
Worker		
Authority		
Provider		
Identity		

Look Back

After completing your Readings and Reflections, and before your group meets this week, take a few moments to look over your readings and reflections: What have you learned? How has God shaped and impacted you? What do you especially want to remember, do, and/or share with your group this week?

Group Discussion

Looking back over this week's personal readings and reflection, discuss at least one or two of the following questions with a close community of friends. As you discuss, remember your commitment to be honest and to help each other "grow up in Christ" by "speaking truth in love" with each other.

1. What concepts were new, or especially stood out, from this week's readings? What was difficult from the readings? What questions do you have from the readings?

2. As a group, how would we together describe this week's three ways of rehearsing the gospel with each other? Which of the ways was most meaningful to you? Which seems the most difficult for you? Why?

This week's Readings and Reflections have taken us a few steps into deeper life together. Even over the past several weeks' group meetings, we have been reminded that God has made us into a people and that we are called to be devoted to each other, and use our gifts, skills, perspectives, and knowledge and love of God for each others' sake.

3. Considering Reflection #1, what are some ways that you have been intentional with the meals you eat, and/or what are some ways you came up with to be even more intentional? Who have you felt compelled to invite to your table and why?

4. Considering Reflection #2, does anyone have any negative views or history with the Lord's Supper that we can help you work through? How can we speak the gospel into that? (If not, simply spend some time discussing how the Lord's Supper is both a remembrance and a declaration of Jesus' death and resurrection.)

5. Considering Reflection #3, can each person share at least one area in which you defined Jesus as "the Better..." in comparison to the human version of that relationship? Are there any areas in which anyone needs help seeing how Jesus is "the Better..." of any of those relationships?

6. Especially in light of this week's community-focused theme, are there any commitments your group needs to make to each other, as you pursue "regularly rehearsing the gospel" in each other's lives together?

Group Exercise

This week's exercise is a little different than previous weeks: you're simply going to celebrate a meal together, and worship God by declaring truths about him that you experience as you eat. You don't have to follow this outline exactly, but here are some suggested conversations your group might have during the meal:

- Everyone might share a sensory experience they've never considered before about the meal.

- Everyone might share one way that their food and drink reminds them of God's goodness.

- Everyone might thank God for a specific element of the meal, the people eating with you, etc.

- Everyone might tell a story about an especially meaningful meal in their lives.

- Everyone might share a way that they've seen this week that Jesus is "the Better," and offer a toast to celebrate him.

After the meal, we'll encourage one of two things, as you honor the convictions and leaders of the church you're a part of...

OPTION 1

If your church tradition encourages communion to be shared in multiple settings, including in community/in homes, have the followers of Jesus among you participate in the Meal: take the Lord's Supper together, with bread and wine (or juice if you prefer). As you do, you might do some of the following:

○ Have someone read 1 Corinthians 11:23-25.

○ As you take the bread and wine, some of you might declare how Jesus' death and resurrection is good news to specific areas of your own life, then partake. (For example: "This week the death and resurrection of Jesus is good news in that it reminds me that in Christ, I am a fully accepted daughter of the Father, with nothing to prove because Jesus' death paid any debt I owed to God.")

○ As you take the bread and wine, some of you might declare how Jesus' death and resurrection is good news to specific areas of others' lives you heard them mention over the meal or throughout previous weeks together, then partake. (For example: "I heard you talk about how the past year has been full of people letting you down and leaving you dissatisfied. In Jesus' death and resurrection, he proves that God always keeps his promises, and one of those promises is that Jesus is the Living Water who will always, fully satisfy you. Let's celebrate that death and life, and the promises and satisfaction it reminds us of, as we take communion together.")

○ As believers take the bread and wine, you might explain to children, or not-yet-believers, the significance of the Lord's Supper, in your own words. (As you do, talk about why Jesus' body was broken and why his blood was shed, and make sure you talk about both Jesus' death and his resurrection, and the promises of God included in both.)

OPTION 2

If your church tradition sees communion as an event to take place on Sundays/with the entire church body gathered, read and discuss how you might keep these themes in mind the next time you participate in the Meal with your broader church family. You might discuss the following:

O Have someone read 1 Corinthians 11:23-25.

O You might declare how Jesus' death and resurrection is good news to specific areas of your own life or each others' lives, or you might explain the significance of the Lord's Supper together. (These elements are further explained in Option 1.)

O Make a plan of how you can each remember and rehearse these things, in your own minds or together, as you take communion the next time your gathered church does so.

NOTE

To better understand and grow in this practice, watch Jeff's missional community share in communion together. Find that video and many more at **saturatethe-world.com/gf**

PRAY

Spend some time praying together, for your group and for each specific person: that God would help you increasingly see all of life—even simple meals—as opportunities to worship him in all you do, that the reality of Jesus' death and resurrection would be more and more real, and that both the Lord's Supper and the words of others would be used by God the Spirit to remind you that Jesus is truly "the Better... (and add specifics as necessary)."

The Gospel With Us

PART 2

WEEK 6

Last week we began looking at tangible ways your community can rehearse gospel truths together. We can speak truth to each other through meals and through the meal. We can speak truth to each other through helping each other see Jesus as "the Better..." in all of life. You've taken a few steps into "speaking the truth in love" to each other in regular ways. This week continues that pattern, as we keep considering "The Gospel with Us." This week's Readings and Reflections give four more practices, by which you and your community can care deeply for one another and lovingly push each other toward Jesus through speaking the gospel into all of life.

Find Jesus in the Story

WEEK 6, READING 1

Thoughtfully read the following excerpts, or for more context and a deeper dive, read the second half of chapter 11 of *Gospel Fluency*, beginning with the section titled "Get to Know the Overall Story."

Another way to grow in seeing Jesus as the Better is to get to know the larger story of the Bible. We walked through a condensed version of it in Week 2. So many people read the Bible as a bunch of individual stories. Sure, there are plenty of stories in the Bible, but the point of the whole Bible is to tell the one true story—the true and better story of the world. It is the story of God and his redeeming love. It is the story of his pursuit of us to rescue and restore us to relation-

172

ships with him, each other, and a renewed creation.

In one sense, the whole Bible is the gospel—the good news that God has come to rescue and restore humanity and all creation in and through the person and work of Jesus Christ. And every part of the Bible either points forward or backward to Jesus, because he is the heart—the center—of the story. The entirety of the Bible also shows how desperately needy every single person is for God's salvation.

Jesus is the point of every story, the fulfillment of every longing, the completion of everything that is lacking. Every character, story, and theme points to him, because it's really all about him. So how can you learn to read the Bible this way? I recommend you go through the story of God together as a group regularly. There are many ways to do this. I am increasingly convinced and concerned that most Christians can't tell the whole story of the Bible. Therefore, they likely can't show how it all leads to Jesus as the Better. I encourage you to take advantage of some of the helpful resources that are available at

saturatetheworld.com to learn the story thoroughly.

I would also strongly encourage you to commit to regularly reading through your Bible—the whole thing. So many Christians have never read their Bibles. Sure, they have favorite sections they read over and over again, but they haven't read the entire book. As a result, most don't know the whole story, so they often wrongly interpret Scripture out of context. When you don't know the whole story of God, you tend toward making the Bible about you and not about Jesus. I would highly recommend that you commit with others to do this. I have found that people are more successful in reading through the entire Bible when they do it with others in their small group or missional community. This allows them to learn together, as well as to hold each other accountable for their reading.

As you get to know your Bible more and more, look to see Jesus in every text by looking for the typology of Jesus in every story or situation. The Bible is not just recounting the story as it occurred, but in such a way as to create an anticipation, a longing, for a better person, a better solution, a better fulfillment—a better Savior. In his providence and through the inspiration of the Holy Spirit, God insured the Scriptures would include numerous "types" (prefigurings) of Christ and would create a vacuum of longing for him to arrive and fulfill our greatest need. Learn to read the Bible, both alone and in community, while asking these questions: **1)** How is this person or situation a type of Christ? **2)** What is lacking in this story that only Jesus can fulfill? and **3)** What is the longing or the hunger that is created here for Jesus to satisfy?

Don't settle for substitutes. Don't try to be a substitute. Jesus did better than anyone or anything. Jesus does better than anyone or anything. And Jesus will do better than anyone or anything. Jesus is the Better everything! Don't look elsewhere and don't give one another anything or anyone else. Remind one another of these truths about him in a gospel-fluent community. And be reminded yourself as you submit to others speaking into your life and experience that Jesus is the Better. Give each other Jesus. He's better.

Thoughtfully read the following passages of Scripture related to today's theme. Take a few moments to write down words and phrases that particularly struck you, as well as any thoughts or personal applications they prompted. Make these words a prayer to God.

Luke 24:13-35

Acts 2:14-41

Acts 17:16-34

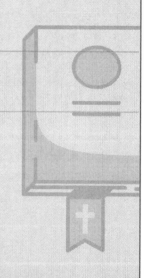

2 Timothy 3:14-17

Find Jesus in the Story

WEEK 6, REFLECTION 1

Reading #1 technically advises two methods of rehearsing the gospel with others: by considering the Story of God (explained in the Introduction), and diving in and reading the whole Bible. The point of both methods, though, is the same: whether you're looking at themes of the Bible or specific texts within it, this week's first way of rehearsing the gospel together is finding Jesus in the story. To apply the concepts of this week's "Reading #1" in your everyday life, pray that God will open your eyes and guide you, then answer the following questions and complete the exercises.

1. Considering the content you read, in your own words describe how you can read the Bible in a way that looks for Jesus as the key to every text. (If you're confused about this—especially regarding the Old Testament, before Jesus was born—ask others to help, or ask your community to talk about it when you meet this week.)

While some followers of Jesus don't seem to know the Bible well, it's also not uncommon in some veins of Christianity today for someone to be "Bible fluent" without being gospel fluent.

Being "Bible fluent" means we know the words, stories, and even commands of Scriptures, and at times we can teach, preach, and even try to obey those words, stories, and commands. "Bible fluency" is a great and needed goal for the Christian life. However, we often become "Bible fluent" without seeing Jesus in the Bible, and without relying on God's gospel work for all that the Bible teaches. By itself, "Bible fluency" leads to moralism (doing good things and living well by our own power), or to guilt and shame (when we fail at doing good and living well by our own power).

For example, Philippians 2:1-11 encourages Christians to be humble toward others; it even looks at the example of Jesus' own humility as a model for our own. Without understanding God's work and the gospel's power in our lives, "Bible fluency" leaves us on our own to follow Jesus' model and become humble. Anyone who's tried this realizes it's a double-edged sword: If we try to become humble on our own, by making our own rules, changing our own mindset, or anything else, we might succeed—but often only for a season, and by the means of self-created legalism. In many cases we ironically end up prideful because of "how humble I've become"! Or we might realize how prideful we are and feel hopeless by our failed efforts which can lead to guilt and shame. Only God, working in us through the truths of the gospel, has the power to make us truly humble: knowing the Bible isn't enough to accomplish that, we need the gospel! Only by trusting in God's power and submitting to the Spirit's work can we truly follow Jesus' example and become more humble.

Knowing the Bible without knowing God and his gospel is not true Christianity. What does it look like to read the Bible through a gospel-fluent lens? In his providence and through the inspiration of the Holy Spirit, God insured the Scriptures would include numerous "types" of Christ and would create a vacuum of longing for him to arrive and fulfill our greatest need. Learn to read the Bible, both alone and in community, while asking these questions: **1)** How is this person or situation a type of Christ? **2)** What is lacking in this story that only Jesus can fulfill? and **3)** What is the longing or the hunger that is created here for Jesus to satisfy?

2. How would you define the differences in "Bible fluency" and "gospel fluency"? Why are both necessary for the Christian life? How is either without the other detrimental?

3. You did this in Week 1, but without looking back, briefly define the gospel. Once you feel good about your definition, look back at Week 1, Reflection 1: how has your definition changed and why?

4. Last week's Reflection #3 asked you to list ways Jesus is "the Better..." in general areas of your own life. Today we'll ask you to do the same, using specific images from the Bible. Pick at least five from the list below: In the first column, write a few words about that biblical person and how he or she did/didn't fulfill his or her role. In the second column, write a few words that describe how Jesus perfectly fulfilled the person's role, in a way they never could, to the glory of God.

JESUS IS THE BETTER ...	HUMAN IN THAT ROLE	JESUS IN THAT ROLE
Adam	*Adam failed the test in the Garden and gave into temptation.*	*Jesus passed the test by overcoming the tempter and submitting himself in the Garden of Gethsemane.*
Abel		
Abraham		
Isaac		
Jacob		
Joseph		
Moses		
Job		
David		
Esther		
Jonah		
For continued development in this skill, compare Jesus to inanimate objects, too: the rock of Moses, manna, the temple, light, water, and more.		

5. As you rest in the fact that Jesus is the key to every theme and text of the Bible, read—and pray that God will help you believe and rest in—this truth: "Jesus is the point of every story, the fulfillment of every longing, the completion of everything that is lacking. Every character, story, and theme points to him, because it's really all about him." Consider writing out your thoughts and prayers as you reflect.

The Hero of Our Story

WEEK 6, READING 2

Thoughtfully read the following excerpts, or for more context and a deeper dive, read the first part of chapter 12 of *Gospel Fluency*, ending before the section titled "Creation."

If you're into film or good fiction, as I am, you can generally discover the hero of the story pretty quickly. The hero generally is brought into the narrative pretty early, with a significant amount of character development designed to draw you in, build your interest in this person, and win you over to [him/]her. Some writers like to keep the hero hidden to create a sense of longing and intrigue, but there still is no doubt by the end who the hero of the story is. The hero stands out above everyone else.

As I listen to many Christians share their stories, I often find that Jesus has become a supporting character, not the hero. Often, a person spends large chunks of time describing his life before meeting Jesus, often going into more detail about his sin than anyone needs to know. Jesus is just a small blip on the radar: "I realized I needed to be forgiven of my sins, and Joe introduced me to Jesus and how he died on the cross for me, so I asked him into my heart." Then the person often goes on to share how hard he has tried to be a better person, but he fails a lot. For instance, he is going to church more often and trying to read his Bible and pray, but life is busy. "Thank God he forgives us!"

By the end of the story, you've heard sin, self, and self-effort, but very little Jesus and very little good news. Often, as in my illustration, the emphasis is on a decision the person made or a welcoming invitation she extended to Jesus. Unfortunately, "I" am the hero of the story. By the way, Jesus doesn't wait for invitations into our hearts. He comes to rescue us from our slavery to sin and Satan. He invades enemy territory, breaks through the stone walls of our hearts, and delivers us from death! He's the hero, not us.

Remember, it is out of the overflow of the heart that the mouth speaks. You talk most about what you love most. My goal in leading a group toward gospel fluency is, first of all, to find out if they know and believe the gospel. If they do, I then want to discover how much their faith in Jesus is shaping their lives. If there is little to no Jesus in their stories, then we need to lay a gospel foundation and pray God grants genuine faith in Jesus.

I use a variety of methods to have people share their stories. Recently, I have used two methods we introduced in the Introduction: "Instagram Stories" (where people draw their story in twelve boxes, then talk us through it using the pictures), and "Three Pillars" (where people reflect on three key events in their lives, which have shaped, influenced, and directed the other elements of their life). The key to these methods—or any method of sharing stories—is to make sure Jesus is the hero. We'll practice that a bit in Reflection #2.

Thoughtfully read the following passages of Scripture related to today's theme. Take a few moments to write down words and phrases that particularly struck you, as well as any thoughts or personal applications they prompted. Make these words a prayer to God.

Luke 24:25-35

John 5:39-40

Acts 2:14-41

The Hero of Our Story

WEEK 6, REFLECTION 2

Reading #2 offers two distinct ways of rehearsing the gospel with others, as covered in the Introduction: we learn to tell our own story, through "Instagram Stories" or through considering "Pillars." The goal of each, as we carry them out in community, is to see Jesus as more and more the hero of our stories, rather than playing a supporting role. To apply the concepts of this week's "Reading #2" in your everyday life, pray that God will open your eyes and guide you, then answer the following questions and complete the exercises.

1. Considering the content you read, think of books, plays, films, and shows: in your own words describe specific ways you can tell who the hero is. Then consider your own life: if you and Jesus were both characters in a book, play, film, or show, what role would others see you each playing?

2. Using the boxes on pages 188–189, tell (or re-tell) your personal "Instagram Story." If you drew and told your "Instagram Story" in your First Meeting, look back: For each frame of the story, do you see Jesus as the hero? Did you tell the story in a way that showed Jesus to be the hero, or did he play a supporting role? If you'd do anything differently after these past several weeks, use the boxes to re-draw your story, and prepare to re-tell it at this week's Group Meeting, with Jesus as the hero of every stage of your story.

    If you chose to tell your First Meeting story using "Pillars," consider using the squares on pages 188–189 to tell your "Instagram Story": each box represents a different part of your story. For each part of the story, draw a still-frame picture that captures the essence of that stage. At this week's group meeting, tell your story using the pictures. It doesn't matter how good your drawings are; this is simply a way for you to tell your story, to share it with others—just make sure Jesus is the hero of each stage of your story!

3. Tell (or re-tell) your story through the image of "Pillars": Here's Jeff's personal experience, as an example of this story-sharing method:

    "In my story, the first pillar is the shame that I experienced as a seventh grader from our pastor when he publicly embarrassed me in front of fifty or more junior high and high school students . . . Unfortunately, since I knew only the good news that Jesus 'saves us from hell,' I didn't know he can also remove our shame in the present. As a result, I looked to myself to deal with shame instead of Jesus. But the only way you can deal with shame apart from Jesus is to perform better and hide more. I tried both. I worked harder at sports, music, and popularity, while I also found more sophisticated ways to hide my sin . . . I didn't run to Jesus for help. I ran from him and everyone else for fear of being found out. I learned how to lead a double life.

"My next pillar is the day when Jesus revealed his love and grace to me while I was in Denia, Spain. In the midst of my sin and shame, he showed up and invited me to surrender my life to him. He revealed to me through the gospel that he knew everything I had done and forgave me for all of it. I knew my guilt was atoned for and my sin was taken away. He saved me and set me free. When I tell my story, I share how Jesus continued to lead me as I learned to follow him through a growing dependence upon him daily.

"Eventually, I get to my third pillar, the time when my people-pleasing idol was revealed in a very painful period of my life. I couldn't keep everyone happy and also do what was right. I was caught, and it led to a time of significant depression. I discovered that it was the loving discipline of our heavenly Father that had brought me to that point. Clearly, I had been saved that day in Spain. However, he wasn't finished with me. He was still saving me. It was during this time that I came to see that Jesus is more powerful than the opinion of man, and that, in Jesus, I had received the approval of God my Father, whose approval matters more than anyone else's.

"Three pillars, three key events. Jesus is the hero."

Jeff's pillars are likely different than yours—but we all have key moments that define our stories. Spend some time asking God to bring to mind three defining moments in your own life, and consider how you would tell your story, based on those three pillars.

If you told your story through "Pillars" in your First Meeting, look back: For each pillar, did you see Jesus as the hero? Did you tell the story in a way that showed Jesus to be the hero, or did he play a supporting role? If you'd do anything differently after these past several weeks, use the pillars on pages 190–191 to re-write your story, and prepare to re-tell it at this week's Group Meeting, with Jesus as the hero of every stage of your story.

4. As you think back through your own story, with both high and low moments and Jesus as your hero, read—and pray that God will help you believe and rest in—this truth: "Remember, it is out of the overflow of the heart that the mouth speaks. You talk most about what you love most. My goal in leading a group toward gospel fluency is, first of all, to find out if they know and believe the gospel. If they do, I then want to discover how much their faith in Jesus is shaping their lives. If there is little to no Jesus in their stories, then we need to lay a gospel foundation and pray God grants genuine faith in Jesus." As you reflect on your story, what emotions, feelings, and beliefs emerge? Consider writing out those insights and taking time to process with God in prayer.

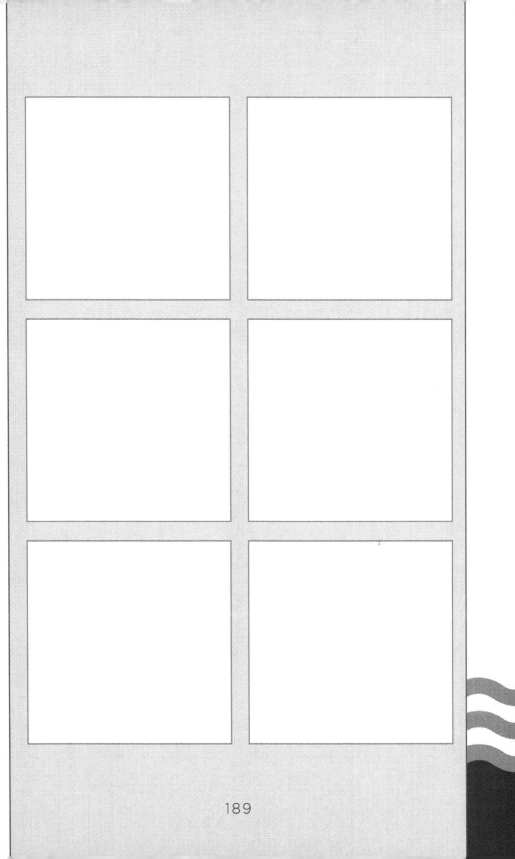

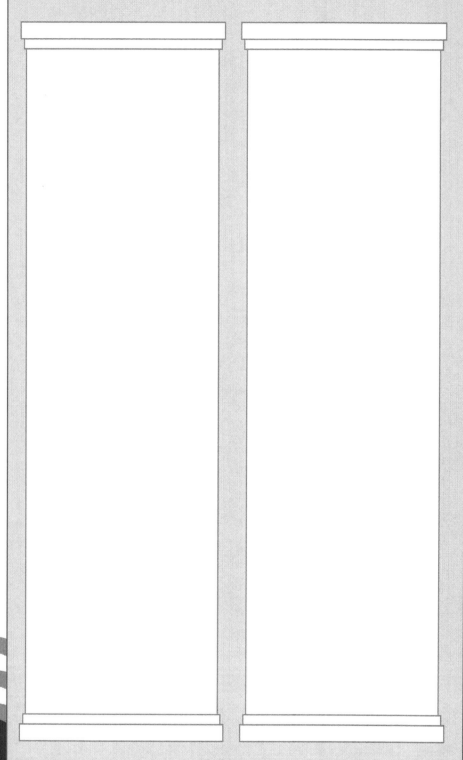

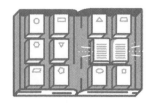

Our Stories in Light of *The* Story

WEEK 6, READING 3

Thoughtfully read the following excerpts, or for more context and a deeper dive, read the second part of chapter 12 of *Gospel Fluency*, starting with the section titled "Creation."

Reflection #2 gave two methods of sharing our personal stories. A third way that we've helped people grow in making Jesus the hero of their stories is by using the four movements of the one true story to help them frame their own: Creation, Fall, Redemption, and New Creation.

CREATION

Creation is all about identity. What do we believe about our origin and purpose? We all have fundamental beliefs about our origins—who or what gave us our existence, made us who we are, and shaped us into the people we are today. We all have learned to find our identity in someone or something. "How did we get here?" and "Why are we here?" are the questions we are answering in this part of our stories. The key question is: "What was my identity in?"

When I teach people how to tell their stories in light of the creation narrative, I encourage them to identify what they looked to or still tend to depend on for their sense of identity. What do they trust for their sense of worth and value? I encourage people to start their stories by talking about their background, some of their early shaping influences, and how these provided a framework for their sense of identity. Remember, the true story grounds our identity in our creation as image-bearers of God, put into the world to represent what he is like in all we do. However, because of sin, we all have been born into brokenness, and the image of God in us is distorted. Also, we have been raised by broken image-bearers who have given us a distorted picture of God, self, and others.

FALL

The fall is about brokenness. In this movement of our stories, we share what has destroyed or is destroying our identity and purpose. The world is not as it should be. We are not as we should be. Brokenness is all around us and in us. Why are things broken? How did we get broken? Who is to blame for our brokenness? These are the kinds of questions people are dealing with in the fall narrative of their stories. The key question is: "Who or what was the problem in my life?"

As I teach people to write their stories in such a way as to make Jesus the hero, I also encourage them to take ownership of their culpability in their brokenness. We all have sinned and fallen short of the glory of God. Identify what you have done that is broken. What have you believed about God, others, and yourself that is wrong? And how have your sinful beliefs led to sinful behaviors? When we tell our stories and fail to confess our sins, we often fail to show our need for a Savior as well. Jesus won't be the hero of the story if we don't really need a Savior for our sin.

REDEMPTION

Redemption is about rescue and deliverance. Everyone is in need of a savior. Everyone needs to be rescued and delivered. This is the part of the story where we share who or what we look to in order to save us or rescue us. The key question is: "Who or what is our savior?"

Everyone is searching for a solution to their problem. For some, it's better friends, spouses, children, or grandchildren. Some look to exercise and diets. Others believe work will save them, or the money they earn from working will do it. Every savior, every solution, ever answer, and every person falls short of addressing our real problem. There is only one Savior who can deal with our real problem of sin, and that is Jesus Christ. At this point of our stories, I encourage people to share who or what they were looking to for deliverance and how they came to see that Jesus is a far better Savior, who rescued and redeemed them from sin and their slavery to it.

NEW CREATION

There is a deep longing in every one of us for change, for transformation, for better—for all things to be made new. Everyone is looking forward to a final conclusion, a complete fulfillment of our every longing, a hopeful climax to our story. This is the happy ending we all long for. And this hope drives us all. We all have things in our hearts and minds that we are expectantly hoping for. In the last part of our stories, we share what has changed in us, as well as the ultimate change we are longing for. We share how we've been transformed and what our ulti-

mate hope is. The key question is: "What has changed and what will change?"

When I instruct people in writing their stories, I encourage them to share how Jesus has and is changing them. I also encourage them to share about their hope for everything to change. The gospel is not just about what has happened. It's also good news about what is happening right now and will happen in the future. We will be saved!

After we hear a person's story, I like to gather the group around the person, lay hands on her if she is okay with that, and pray, giving thanks to God for the work of Jesus in her life. The story should declare Jesus to be the hero, and then we should give thanks in prayer to Jesus for being the hero of our stories. Gospel fluency is developed both in sharing our stories and in thanking the one who wrote them.

Thoughtfully read the following passages of Scripture related to today's theme. Take a few moments to write down words and phrases that particularly struck you, as well as any thoughts or personal applications they prompted. Make these words a prayer to God.

Acts 17:22-31

Colossians 1:15-23

(And, you might read Genesis 1-3 again and look specifically for the story themes.)

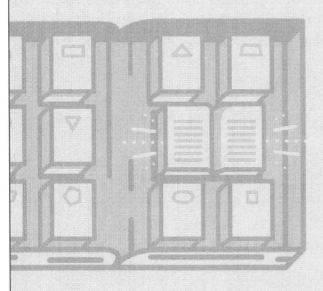

Our Stories in Light of *The* Story

WEEK 6, REFLECTION 3

A final way for your community to rehearse the gospel regularly with each other is to see our own stories through the lenses of *the* story, the Story of God. To apply the concepts of this week's "Reading #3" in your everyday life, pray that God will open your eyes and guide you, then answer the following questions and complete the exercises. For each lens below, we give you an example and then a general scenario to practice, and ask that you add a third (or more), specific to your own life.

1. Consider your story through the lens of "creation": The key question is "What is my identity in?" Identify what you look to or tend to depend on for your sense of identity. What do you trust for your sense of worth and value? What has this looked like at different points of your life? If you're a follower of Jesus, what changed about your identity after he saved you?

   O An entry-level employee with a difficult boss:
   might find his/her identity in his/her job, title, boss's approval, money, success, or proving him/herself

   O A person struggling with his/her singleness:

   O Your own story:

2. Consider your story through lens of "fall": The fall is about brokenness. The key question is: "Who or what was the problem in my life?" Often when what you look to for your sense of identity (your creation stories) fails you, that is what you blame. Sometimes your perceived problem is the culture around you or the failure of friends or coworkers. And sometimes you see yourself as the problem. What has this looked like at different points of your life? If you're a follower of Jesus, what changed as you realized the true problem is sin—our unbelief in God?

   - An entry-level employee with a difficult boss:
     might see losing his/her job or messing up a big account as the greatest problem, or might see his/her lack of ability or skills, the boss' attitude or bias, or the concept of work as a whole as the reason the boss is difficult

   - A person struggling with his/her singleness:

   - Your own story:

3. Consider your story through the lens of "redemption": Redemption is about rescue and deliverance. The key question is: "Who or what is our savior?" Think about who or what you are looking to for deliverance and whether you have come to see that Jesus is a far better Savior, who rescued and redeemed you from sin and your slavery to it. What has this looked like at different points of your life? If you're a follower of Jesus, what has changed since you've seen Jesus as your one true Savior?

   o An entry-level employee with a difficult boss:
      might look for "salvation" through workaholism, perfectionism, cheating his/her way to the top, putting aside convictions to be noticed or approved of; the boss, performance, or self become the functional savior

   o A person struggling with his/her singleness:

   o Your own story:

4. Consider your story through the lens of "new creation": There is a deep longing in every one of us for change, for transformation, for better—for all things to be made new. The key question is: "What has changed and what will change?" We were created for more. Our present reality appears distant from the life and world we desire. Everyone longs for a new creation. So, what is our version of the new creation? What has this looked like at different points of your life? If you're a follower of Jesus, how has he changed you? How has he given you a better, ultimate hope?

○ An entry-level employee with a difficult boss:
hope might be found in the boss's approval, in feeling good about the job, in self-reliance, achievement, or in financial gain/ reward

○ A person struggling with his/her singleness:

○ Your own story:

5. As you think through your own story through these four lenses, remember Jeff's encouragement to his communities as they share stories: "After we hear a person's story, I like to gather the group around the person, lay hands on him/her if they are okay with that, and pray, giving thanks to God for the work of Jesus in their life. The story should declare Jesus to be the hero, and then we should give thanks in prayer to Jesus for being the hero of our stories. Gospel fluency is developed both in sharing our stories and in thanking the one who wrote them." Consider writing out your thoughts and prayers as you reflect.

Look Back

After completing your Readings and Reflections, and before your group meets this week, take a few moments to look over your readings and reflections: What have you learned? How has God shaped and impacted you? What do you especially want to remember, do, and/or share with your group this week?

Group Discussion

Looking back over this week's personal readings and reflection, discuss at least one or two of the following questions with a close community of friends. As you discuss, remember your commitment to be honest and to help each other "grow up in Christ" by "speaking truth in love" with each other.

1. What concepts were new, or especially stood out, from this week's readings? What was difficult from the readings? What questions do you have from the readings?

2. As a group, how would we together describe this week's four ways of rehearsing the gospel with each other? Which of the ways was most meaningful to you? Which seems the most difficult for you? Why?

There are, of course, innumerable ways to rehearse the gospel in community in meaningful ways. The goal of this week and last was to help you and your group take a few "first steps" into practicing that vital part of the Christian life. This week's Readings and Reflections have given us four ways to rehearse the gospel, as we consider how Jesus is the hero of our own lives and stories.

3. Did anything from Reading and Reflection #1, about seeing Jesus as the key to every theme and text of the Bible, strike you as new, impacting, or convicting? Was anything about that concept difficult, or is there anything our community can help anyone with regarding that?

4. Which exercises were easier and which were more difficult? In what ways was it easy for each of us to tell various forms of our stories in a way that showed Jesus to be the hero, and in what ways was it difficult? Why? (Follow-up: Does anyone have any questions about these methods or need any encouragement regarding this week's exercises?)

5. Does anyone feel as though—this week or in previous weeks—you've understood the gospel in a new way, or even truly for the first time? If so, how can our community love and support each other as we understand and pursue this new, or "reawakened," faith? Does anyone need to be baptized, as God continues to work in our stories?

6. Especially in light of this week's community-focused theme, are there any commitments your group needs to make to each other as you pursue "regularly rehearsing the gospel" together?

Group Exercise

This week's exercise invites each person to share their stories[1], through one of the ways you practiced in this week's Readings and Reflections. Nothing has to be perfect; this isn't a presentation—it's merely a way of celebrating God's work in each others' lives, and especially celebrating Jesus, the true hero of each of our stories.

It's ideal for the entire group to hear each other's stories, so you might want to take two weeks to carry out this exercise. Or you may want to divide into groups of three or four, to make sure everyone gets a chance to participate.

First, have each person...

O   Share their stories through one of the methods practiced this week: Instagram Stories, Pillars, or "Creation - Fall - Redemption - New Creation." You might limit this to 10 minutes (or less, depending on the size of the group).

After each person shares, together as a group...

O   Celebrate ways you heard God working in each person's life story.

O   Encourage each person in their growing gospel fluency, and ways they were able to clearly point to Jesus as the hero of various parts of their stories.

O   Gather around the person, lay hands on him/her if he/she is okay with that, and pray, giving thanks to God for the work of Jesus in his/her life. Just as the story declared Jesus to be the hero, so should we give thanks in prayer to Jesus for being the hero of our stories.

---

1. For an additional resource in learning to tell your story, listening to others' stories, and connecting our stories with THE story, visit **saturatetheworld.com/gf**

PRAY

Spend some time praying for your group together; that God would help each person see their own stories—the beautiful moments and the broken moments—as gifts from him. And pray that God the Spirit would use our own stories to consistently encourage each other and point us toward Jesus, and that Jesus would continually be more and more the hero, in our own minds and in the stories we tell and believe.

The Gospel to Others

PART 1

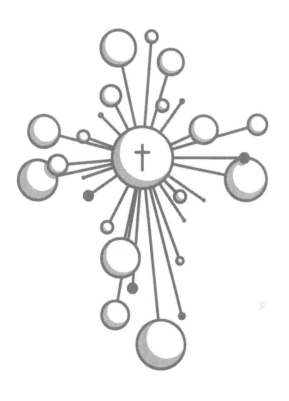

WEEK 7

This week we enter the final section of *Gospel Fluency*, turning our gaze to "The Gospel to Others." The good news of Jesus is not just for those who already follow him, but is good news for everyone, and is the means through which people begin following Jesus. This week's Readings and Reflections center around listening and learning, and displaying the gospel in meaningful ways to those around us who don't yet follow Jesus as their Lord.

Listen & Learn

WEEK 7, READING 1

Thoughtfully read the following excerpts, or for more context and a deeper dive, read the first part of chapter 13 of *Gospel Fluency*, ending before the section titled "Listening Up."

I recently observed a conversation a few Christians were having with a man who has yet to come to faith in Jesus. It was amazing to me, and saddening, to watch the Christians missing the point of this man's struggle and questions. It seemed those speaking to him were more concerned about convincing him they were right than about listening to his heart. As a result, he walked away without any good news about Jesus, becoming even more con-vinced that this "religion" wasn't for him.

It's not for me either—at least, not what I saw in that conversation. We can do better. We must do better. We're talking about people's souls! And we're representing Jesus. Gospel fluency isn't just about talking. It's about listening as well. This requires love, patience, and wisdom. I've found that starting with a posture of humility, standing in a place of need, and having a heart that is willing not just to give answers but to receive insight creates a welcoming place for people to open their hearts. The more open we are to listen and learn, the more likely people are to be open as well.

[Jesus is] a master at drawing out the heart. You notice this if you read the Gospels. Jesus regularly said just enough to invite further probing or create intrigue. He also loved to ask questions so that the overflow of the heart (belief) would spill out of a person's mouth (words).

I'm amazed at how often well-intentioned Christians overwhelm people with a barrage of words. We go on and on about what we believe and what they should believe, assuming we know what others think, believe, or need. I often find that we are giving answers to questions people are not even asking or cramming information into hearts that are longing for love, not just facts. We fail to listen. We fail to draw out the heart. And we miss opportunities to really love people and share the love of God with them. They also miss out on getting to hear what's going on in their own hearts. I have found that when people, including myself, are invited to say out loud what they believe, they come to realize something is wrong.

As we are changed by the gospel, we want to share how the gospel has changed us. It's a great thing to do so. In fact, one of the keys to growing in gospel fluency is to regularly share what Jesus has done or is doing in our lives with others. Our stories are powerful demonstrations of the gospel's power to save.

However, if we don't also listen, we tend to share the good news of Jesus in a way that applies primarily to our lives, the way it was good news to us, but fails to address the situations others are facing. We can become proclaimers of good news while being ignorant of the ways in which others need to hear it. This doesn't negate how good the news of Jesus is at all.

Our job is to testify to Jesus' work in our lives while also listening closely to others so we know how to bring the truths of Jesus to bear on the longings of their hearts. We need to bring them to Jesus so he can meet their unique needs—fulfill their personal longings. In order to do this, we have to slow down, quiet our souls, ask good questions to draw out the hearts of others, and listen. Francis Schaeffer was known to say, "If I have only an hour with someone, I will spend the first fifty-five minutes asking them questions and finding out what is troubling their heart and mind, and then in the last five minutes I will share something of the truth."[2]

My regular counsel to Christians these days is to spend more time listening than talking if they want to be able to share the gospel of Jesus in a way that meaningfully speaks to the hearts of others. We all long for Jesus Christ. Everyone is seeking him, even if they don't know it. They are looking for something to fulfill their longings and satisfy their thirst. However, they are likely looking in the wrong places. They are going to the wrong wells to try to draw soul water. They need to look to Jesus. But they will not come to see how he can quench their thirst if we don't take the time to listen.

And as we listen, with the help of the Holy Spirit, we can discern the longings of their hearts, the brokenness of their souls, the emptiness of their spirits. And then, we must be prepared to show how Jesus can meet them at the well with soul-quenching water—himself.

Thoughtfully read the following passages of Scripture related to today's theme. Take a few moments to write down words and phrases that particularly struck you, as well as any thoughts or personal applications they prompted. Make these words a prayer to God.

Proverbs 20:5

Ecclesiastes 3:11

John 4:1-30

2. Footnote from original GF book: Cited in Jerram Barrs, introduction to Francis A. Schaeffer, He Is There and He Is Not Silent, 30th Anniversary Edition (Wheaton, IL: Tyndale House, 2001), xviii.

Listen & Learn

WEEK 7, REFLECTION 1

To apply the concepts of this week's "Reading #1" in your everyday life, pray that God will open your eyes and guide you, then answer the following questions and complete the exercises.

1. Find a crowded public place to sit for awhile this week (such as a coffee shop, pub, park, etc). Spend time there, and simply listen to conversations going on around you. While you listen or after you leave, write down parts of the conversations that stand out to you. Reflect on them, in light of the gospel and story of God we've been considering: How do conversations you heard fall in line with the gospel? How do they depart from it? If you were engaged in the conversation what might you have said and why?

2. Write the names of at least three people you consider close friends (not acquaintances or co-workers you only see in the office—those who are truly friends), who don't follow Jesus:

3. For each of the three friends whose names you wrote above, think through a recent conversation in which you've talked about heart level stuff (what they believe, are struggling with, etc.). If you haven't had a conversation with a non-believing friend recently, take some time this week to do so and slow down to ask good questions and listen. Summarize each in a sentence or two below. (Example: What did you talk about? Did you hear their heart speak through their words or struggles? What do you think they believe about God and self? What did you say and what did they say? How did the conversation end?)

4. If we don't also listen, we tend to share the good news of Jesus in a way that applies primarily to our lives, the way it was good news to us, but fails to address the situations others are facing. We can become proclaimers of good news while being ignorant of the ways in which others need to hear it. In Week 2, we asked you to mention the "angle of the gospel" that made it seem like truly good news to you. Look back (pgs. 78, 90 in #4, and 168) and write your answers below. Then, for each of the three friends you listed above, list a few areas of sin, disbelief, struggle, or question in which the gospel might be good news to each.

5. As you think back through the way the gospel became good news to you, and the way it might become good news to specific non-believing friends, read—and pray that God will help you believe and rest in—this truth: "We all long for Jesus Christ. Everyone is seeking him, even if they don't know it. They are looking for something to fulfill their longings and satisfy their thirst. However, they are likely looking in the wrong places. They are going to the wrong wells to try to draw soul water. They need to look to Jesus. But they will not come to see how he can quench their thirst if we don't take the time to listen." Write out your thoughts as you consider these ideas and turn them into prayers as you reflect.

Listen in Light of the Story

WEEK 7, READING 2

Thoughtfully read the following excerpts, or for more context and a deeper dive, read the second part of chapter 13 of *Gospel Fluency*, beginning with the section titled "Listening Up."

Whenever I am engaging in a conversation with someone, I ask the Holy Spirit to help me. He is called "the Helper," after all (John 14:26). "Help me slow down," I pray. "Help me to trust you are working here in the silence. Help me to listen well—to them and to you." In some Bible versions, "Helper" is translated as "Counselor." So I ask the Spirit to give me the ability to hear the longings of the heart as I listen. I invite him to be the primary counselor in the midst of our time. I ask him to give me ears to hear what the real issues are, and then provide me with wisdom as to how to share the truths of Jesus in such a way that they will be good news to the other person.

I am more and more convinced that the Holy Spirit goes ahead of us, preparing people for conversations like this. This growing confidence in God as the one who saves has freed me from the pressure to be the savior for people. Our job is to be present, filled with the Spirit, and ready to listen, then open to speak as the Spirit leads.

As you grow in listening to people's longings, also learn to listen for their overarching stories. [In last week's Readings and Reflections], I described how we can share our stories, making Jesus the hero. If we are going to speak the gospel fluently to the hearts of others, we need to listen for the dominant storylines under which others live their lives. What are their gospel stories? Who's their hero? Let's look at the fundamental questions or longings in each movement of the story in light of people God has put in our lives. Get familiar with them, and then, as you listen to people, listen for their answers to the questions:

- **Creation:** In what do they find their identity or sense of purpose and significance?

- **Fall:** Who or what is the fundamental problem they blame for the things that are broken in their lives?

- **Redemption:** Who or what are they looking to as their savior to rescue or deliver them?

- **New Creation:** What does transformation look like and what is their ultimate hope for the future?

In *Gospel Fluency* chapter 13, Jeff shares the Spirit's work in helping him hear two peoples' stories, and how he was able to share the gospel in meaningful ways to both. Here's a brief overview of each conversation. In the first, a woman on a plane who revealed that she was in the process of a divorce, described how she had had an affair and how her husband, in his anger, had done everything he could to destroy her image on Facebook, turning all their friends against her. He had succeeded in turning her sons against her as well. She was terribly embarrassed, broken, and demoralized. I listened for quite some time, and it became clear to me that she was sorry for what she had done and regretted the pain and shame it had brought on her and her family. And she was deeply burdened by her husband's anger and her sons' pain.

Over the course of a long conversation, I shared with the woman that she was feeling shame and guilt because of her sin and her subsequent attempts to deal with it. I shared with her the story of Adam and Eve, and how they tried to deal with their sin. I continued to show her how it led them to blame each other and brought destruction in their relationships. "What you need," I continued, "is one who can truly atone for your sin. You need someone who can handle the weight of sin, forgive you of your sin, and set you free from it, so that it no longer defines you. You need Jesus."

I then went on to describe how Jesus willingly went to the cross to take her sin on himself. I shared how he was willing to be publicly shamed for her so that she not only could be forgiven, but also clothed in his righteousness and freed from guilt and shame. We went on and on about how the gospel brings forgiveness, healing, hope, and even love for those we've hurt or been hurt by.

She wanted to make things right. She wanted forgiveness, healing, and reconciliation. Jesus had good news for her. I let her know that I know and love Jesus, and that Jesus cared and was listening to her as well. She then shared how she had never been into religion, but recently she had been seeking and checking out some churches in our area. She knew she needed help and was reaching out.

In the second example, a friend was lamenting his recent job loss. Over the course of a long conversation, he admitted that his identity had been tied to his job: "without it, I'm not sure who I am anymore." After sharing a similar situation from his own life, Jeff prodded his friend to share more about his upbringing, and learned that the young man had lost his father during his teenage years. In hearing more of the man's story, the Spirit helped Jeff listen and realize the following:

What was his Creation narrative? "My identity is in my job because I'm looking for approval and love from my dad." What was his Fall narrative? "My dad died and I lost my job. And even though I could get another job, I could lose it as well. Nothing is dependable. Nothing lasts. We lose dads and jobs." What was his Redemption narrative? "I need a dad who will love me and a job well done." What was his New Creation narrative? "I want a dad who won't die and will be proud of my work."

Do you see how the gospel has great news for my friend? With the Spirit's help, I did. So I gave it to him. Both conversations are merely summarized here for the sake of brevity, and thus lack nuance and most of the words in each conversation. We'll say again, that both are given more context and fleshed out more in *Gospel Fluency*. But at the end of the day, [everyone needs] the good news of Jesus shared as good news for [each of our specific areas of] pain and longing. Remember, we don't save people. God does. We listen and learn, and then we love and share Jesus.

Thoughtfully read the following passages of Scripture related to today's theme. Take a few moments to write down words and phrases that particularly struck you, as well as any thoughts or personal applications they prompted. Make these words a prayer to God.

John 14:26

Galatians 5:22-25

Look again at how the Apostle Paul spoke to direct areas of need and question in Acts 17:16-34.

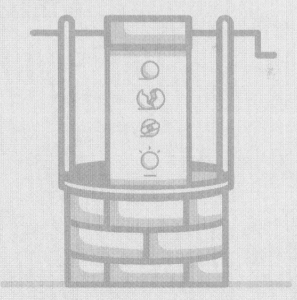

Listen in Light of the Story

WEEK 7, REFLECTION 2

To apply the concepts of this week's "Reading #2" in your everyday life, pray that God will open your eyes and guide you, then answer the following questions and complete the exercises.

1. In chapter 13 of *Gospel Fluency*, Jeff writes, "As we listen, with the help of the Holy Spirit, we can discern the longings of their hearts, the brokenness of their souls, the emptiness of their spirits. And then, we must be prepared to show how Jesus can meet them at the well with soul-quenching water—himself." Considering the ways you wrote down in Reflection #1 that the gospel might become good news to each of your non-believing friends, take some time to pray that God might show you specific ways you might "speak truth in love" with each. Write down a few ways Jesus might answer some of the questions/needs your friends have.

2. Each of the non-Christian friends you mentioned in Reflection #1 believes some story. If it's not the gospel story, they're believing a lesser story. Considering what you know of your friends, answer the following questions for each:

FRIEND #1

○ **Creation**: In what do they find their identity or sense of purpose and significance?

○ **Fall**: Who or what is the fundamental problem they blame for the things that are broken in their lives?

○ **Redemption**: Who or what are they looking to as their savior to rescue or deliver them?

○ **New Creation**: What does transformation look like, and what is their ultimate hope for the future?

FRIEND #2

○ **Creation**: In what do they find their identity or sense of purpose and significance?

○ **Fall**: Who or what is the fundamental problem they blame for the things that are broken in their lives?

○ **Redemption**: Who or what are they looking to as their savior to rescue or deliver them?

○ **New Creation**: What does transformation look like, and what is their ultimate hope for the future?

FRIEND #3

- **Creation**: In what do they find their identity or sense of purpose and significance?

- **Fall**: Who or what is the fundamental problem they blame for the things that are broken in their lives?

- **Redemption**: Who or what are they looking to as their savior to rescue or deliver them?

- **New Creation**: What does transformation look like, and what is their ultimate hope for the future?

3. After considering your friends' stories in light of *the* story, what might be a few specific ways you might share the story—their true identity in Christ, sin as the ultimate problem, Jesus as the one true savior, or the fullness of hope in God alone?

4. To put this week's theory into practice, prayerfully consider taking a bold step, trusting God and the leading of the Spirit, and have a conversation with at least one of those non-believing friends, in which you share the gospel through one of the ways discussed in questions #1-3.

5. As you think back through your own story through these four lenses, read—and pray that God will help you believe and rest in—this truth: "Whenever I am engaging in a conversation with someone, I ask the Holy Spirit to help me. He is called 'the Helper,' after all (John 14:26) . . . In some Bible versions, 'Helper' is translated as 'Counselor.' So I ask the Spirit to give me the ability to hear the longings of the heart as I listen. I invite him to be the primary counselor in the midst of our time. I ask him to give me ears to hear what the real issues are, and then provide me with wisdom as to how to share the truths of Jesus in such a way that they will be good news to the other person." As you reflect on this, write out your thoughts and spend some time talking to God about it in prayer.

Display the Gospel

WEEK 7, READING 3

Thoughtfully read the following excerpts, or for more context and a deeper dive, read the first part of chapter 14 of Gospel Fluency, ending with the section titled "Declare."

In the true story, we learn that God has always intended to have a visible representation of himself on the earth. Adam and Eve failed. Then Israel failed. But Jesus did not. He is the true image of God— the fullness of deity in bodily form. Now, we, the church, are his body, the means by which he intends to fill every place with his embodied presence through our physical bodies (Eph. 1:22–23). We were not just saved from sin, Satan, and death. We were also saved for his purposes here and now.

Saved from and saved for. We were saved by the power of God for the purposes of God, so that God might be made known and

Jesus might be glorified. We are God's display people, showing the world what he is like. We are also a declaration people, who proclaim who God is and what he has done by proclaiming the gospel. Reading and Reflection #3 focuses on the "display" side of this, and next week's final Readings and Reflections turn to the "declaration" side.

In 1 Peter 2:9-15, Peter [tells] God's people scattered throughout Asia Minor (modern-day Turkey) that they were called to live as God's chosen people who loved others like family, just as God the Father had loved them while they were still his enemies. They were his royal priesthood, sent into the world by the Spirit to help people be reconciled to God and to each other through Jesus. And they were a holy nation, called to display what life can be like when Jesus is King. So are we. This is our identity. This is our calling.

Show the world the love of the Father, the healing and reconciling power of the Spirit, and the sacrificial servanthood of the Son in how you live. Show them what God is like.

It has been said that behavior is more caught than taught. Every parent knows this to be true. Our children more often reflect what we do in front of them than what we say to them. The display of our lives is definitely more convincing than the declaration of our lips. In fact, if we say one thing and do another, our doing often trumps what we say in people's minds. So what are we displaying to the world?

From time to time, I've led groups to embrace the practice of being a gospel display through an activity I call "Gospel Metaphors." I encourage the group members to think about the gospel and what we come to know about God through

Jesus' work. Then I invite them to share the titles, attributes, and activities of God that we see in Jesus. Advocate. Sacrifice. Healer. Forgiver. Counselor. Prince of Peace. Restorer. Redeemer. The list could go on and on. While people are sharing, I write the words down on a whiteboard or poster-sized Post-it note. Often, many suggestions are given. And I usually select a few additional attributes or titles and ask how we could provide [a] picture of what God is like in those ways.

The apostle Paul said we are like living letters displaying the work of God to the world—gospel metaphors. As a result of an exercise such as this, I've witnessed fences repaired (Restorer); houses remodeled to make more space for people in need of places to stay (Hospitable); an empty lot that was used for drug and sex trafficking transformed into a community garden (Redeemer); debts paid off (Forgiver); college tuition raised (Provider); fatherless children cared for by men (Father to the fatherless); and many other displays of the character of God. Small and big activities alike can display what God is like, as we've come to know him in the gospel.

We are blessed by God to bless. Physical displays of what God is like show his glory in tangible form.

Thoughtfully read the following passages of Scripture related to today's theme. Take a few moments to write down words and phrases that particularly struck you, as well as any thoughts or personal applications they prompted. Make these words a prayer to God.

Read the book of 1 Peter. See this week's themes through the progression of Peter's letter: Peter begins with the gospel, explains the principle of living as God's "display community," then gives specific examples of how that can look in different situations.

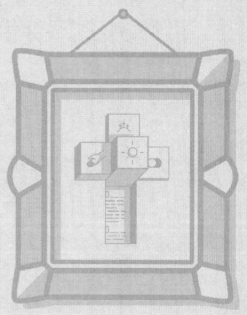

Display the Gospel

To apply the concepts of this week's "Reading #2" in your everyday life, pray that God will open your eyes and guide you, then answer the following questions and complete the exercises.

1. Read 1 Peter 2:9-12. Peter says to God's people scattered throughout Asia Minor (modern-day Turkey), "But you are a chosen race, a royal priesthood, a holy nation, a people for his own possession, that you may proclaim the excellencies of him who called you out of darkness into his marvelous light" (1 Pet. 2:9). Then, in verse 12, he adds, "Keep your conduct among the Gentiles honorable, so that when they speak against you as evildoers, they may *see your good deeds* and *glorify God* on the day of visitation. [italics added]" Why is it important for us to both display and declare the gospel?

2. 1 Peter 2:11 paints a picture of two extremes that Christians are commonly drawn toward: on one extreme, we can not only "abstain" from sin (which is biblical) but go too far and try and abstain from "sinners" (which is unbiblical). On the other extreme, we can go beyond living "among" the Gentiles (at the time, Gentiles were anyone who didn't know God), to living "like" them (which is unbiblical). The biblical call lands in the middle of the pendulum: our charge as we display the gospel is to live holy lives unto God, but do so publicly, in the context of meaningful relationships with non-believers. That's a life of pursuing God, lived "among" those who don't follow God.

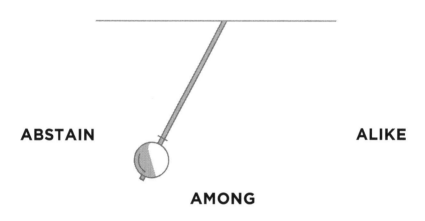

ABSTAIN   **ALIKE**

AMONG

Which extreme on the pendulum do you tend toward? What motives (both good and poor) draw you toward that extreme? How might you need to apply the gospel to that?

3. In the first column on the next page, write some biblical commands God gives his people in the Bible. In other words, who are God's people called to be, and how does God command us to display the gospel? In the second column, explain how each command reflects who God is and what he does. In the third, explain how God clearly modeled the command in the life, death, and resurrection of Jesus. Then in the final column, write some of the results in the Bible as God's people both did and didn't fulfill those commands. We give you one example.

GOD'S COMMAND IN THE BIBLE (Who are God's people called to be and how are they/we to live?)	HOW DOES IT REFLECT WHO GOD IS AND WHAT GOD DOES?
Love your enemies and pray for those who persecute you.	God is a Father; he created all humankind in his image; "God is love"; he is the chief "forgiver"; he pursues people even while they reject him.

HOW DOES THE GOSPEL CLEARLY MODEL/FULFILL THIS COMMAND?	BIBLICAL RESULTS OF GOD'S PEOPLE OBEYING/ DISOBEYING GOD'S COMMAND
Jesus prayed for Jerusalem and asked God to forgive those who were killing him. He died for the sins of all people—even those who opposed him; his sacrificial death was the greatest act of love in history.	obeying: reconciliation, forgiveness, unity, blessing (like Jesus with Peter or Joseph with his brothers), salvation; disobeying: division, strife, bitterness, and division ("hardened hearts"); we're only forgiven as we forgive

4. In chapter 14 of *Gospel Fluency*, Jeff writes about the idea of "gospel metaphors": "I encourage the group members to think about the gospel and what we come to know about God through Jesus' work. Then I invite them to share the titles, attributes, and activities of God that we see in Jesus.

"Advocate. Sacrifice. Healer. Forgiver. Counselor. Prince of Peace. Restorer. Redeemer. The list could go on and on.

"While people are sharing, I write the words down on a whiteboard or poster-sized Post-it note.

"Then I pick one. If I choose Restorer, I say: 'We have been blessed to be a blessing. God has shown us what he is like by what he has done for us. Now we get to show the world what he is like by what we do for them. So, how might we show how God brings restoration through Jesus in our neighborhood or community together?'

"Some of the responses have been:

- 'Well, we could walk the neighborhood together in prayer, asking the Spirit to show us what is broken and needs repair, then offer to repair it.'

- 'We could lead a study that we open up to the community on how to deal with conflict in our relationships.'

- 'What if we start with everyone in the group? Do we have brokenness here that needs to be dealt with? How are our relationships doing? How are our hearts doing? Let's make sure we are experiencing it ourselves first.'

"As a result of an exercise such as this, I've witnessed fences repaired (Restorer); houses remodeled to make more space for people in need of places to stay (Hospitable); an empty lot that was used for drug and sex trafficking transformed into a community garden (Redeemer); debts paid off (Forgiver); college tuition raised (Provider); fatherless children cared for by men (Father to the fatherless); and many other displays of the character of God. Small and big activities alike can display what God is like, as we've come to know him in the gospel.

"We are blessed by God to bless. Physical displays of what God is like show his glory in tangible form."

In preparation for your group's meeting this week, consider the titles given to Jesus in Jeff's example, and add a few of your own. For at least three, write one or two ways you could put that attribute on display in tangible, everyday ways:

ATTRIBUTE	HOW CAN WE DISPLAY IN TANGIBLE, EVERYDAY WAYS?
Advocate	
Sacrifice	
Healer	
Forgiver	
Counselor	
Prince of Peace	
Restorer	
Redeemer	

5. As you consider various ways to display the gospel to others, read—and pray that God will help you believe and rest in—this truth: "This is our calling. Show the world the love of the Father, the healing and reconciling power of the Spirit, and the sacrificial servanthood of the Son in how you live. Show them what God is like." Write out your thoughts as you consider these ideas and turn them into prayers as you reflect.

Look Back

After completing your Readings and Reflections, and before your group meets this week, take a few moments to look over your readings and reflections: What have you learned? How has God shaped and impacted you? What do you especially want to remember, do, and/or share with your group this week?

Group Discussion

Looking back over this week's personal readings and reflection, discuss at least one or two of the following questions with a close community of friends. As you discuss, remember your commitment to be honest and to help each other "grow up in Christ" by "speaking truth in love" with each other.

1. What concepts were new, or especially stood out, from this week's readings? What was difficult from the readings? What questions do you have from the readings?

2. As a group, how would we together describe the importance of listening to others, relying on God the Spirit to help us know how to speak the gospel into their stories, and displaying the gospel?

This week was about listening, learning, and displaying. As we talk about these areas more, let's remember that we rely on God the Spirit to teach us about our non-believing friends, and that it's only God who can produce any fruit in our displays of the gospel.

3. What did you learn—about others, your friends, or even yourself—as you simply took the time to stop, listen, and consider conversations you've heard or had through the lens of the gospel?

4. In light of your reflections, what were some meaningful ways you thought of to show the good news of Jesus visibly or to verbally share the good news with some of your non-believing friends? Did you do either? If so, what did you do? How can this community help you see their story in light of *the* story, and how can we encourage and embolden you to share the good news of Jesus with a friend?

5. What were some of the gospel metaphors you came up with through which the gospel can be put on display? Tell us about ways you've carried out one or two of these this week.

6. Especially related to helping each other carry out God's mission of making disciples, are there any commitments your group needs to make to each other as you pursue "regularly rehearsing the gospel" in each other's lives together?

Group Exercise

This week's exercise is two-fold; you'll likely be able to keep the entire group together for both halves.

1. First, as you consider displaying the gospel to the world as a community, make some plans, to be carried out during your meeting or some other time before you meet again:

   o Are there meaningful metaphors our group can commit to pursuing together?

   o Whether we actively meet and display the gospel together, or our whole group simply commits to carry out certain practices on our own, when/how can we display each metaphor we list?

2. Second, take a few moments to pray for God to help you share the gospel:

   o Start by discussing God's role—and our dependency on the Spirit—as our "helper" in making disciples.

   o Then take at least 10 minutes to pray:

      • Spend some time looking over this week's reflection questions related to your friends who don't know Jesus. Especially consider the needs you heard and ways their heart might need to be drawn out.

- As you consider what you've heard and learned from them, the story they live, and ways you might share the gospel with them, ask God the Spirit to help you: Maybe you want to ask him to help you know them, listen to them, or understand them. Maybe you want to ask him to reveal needs or questions they have. Maybe you need help knowing how to share the good news. Or a hundred other things. Be patient and still before God, and spend some time in corporate prayer together.

- Once you finish, consider sharing some things that stuck out from your prayer time.

- And the big action step as you leave, especially given next week's topic, is to boldly, lovingly, and winsomely share the gospel with someone who doesn't follow Jesus, this coming week.

✱NOTE✱

Enrich your learning and experience for this week by watching the companion video at **saturatetheworld.com/gf**

PRAY

Spend some time praying together, for your group and for each specific person. Pray that God would help each person slow down and listen—to God, to others, and in light of this week, to non-believing friends. Pray that he would empower you with boldness and the words you need to share the good news in meaningful ways and that he would help give you the desire and discipline to live a holy life "among the Gentiles," as you display God to an unbelieving world.

The Gospel to Others

PART 2

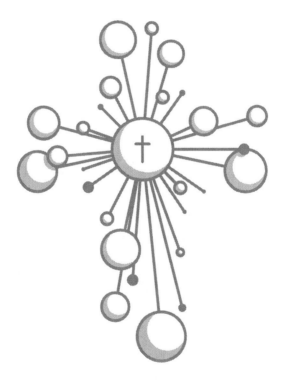

WEEK 8

Our final week together brings us to some of the most difficult aspects of the Christian life. As we look again at "The Gospel to Others," we dive into actually sharing the gospel, with our words, to those who don't know Jesus. But our words are only meaningful if we consider the heart behind them: so while we consider our gospel declaration this week, we end our eight-week journey by looking at our hearts, and our own need for God's love and wisdom.

Declare the Gospel

WEEK 8, READING 1

Thoughtfully read the following excerpts, or for more context and a deeper dive, read the second part of chapter 14 of *Gospel Fluency*, beginning with the section titled "Declare."

I've found that when we live our lives intentionally as display people, we get plenty of opportunities to talk about why we do it. Lives full of grace and love; schedules rearranged to make space to listen and serve; budgets adjusted to feed and care for people; or words spoken to protect and build up all demand explanations. These things really don't make sense apart from the gospel. Yet in our explanations to others, we so often forget to give them Jesus.

Paul says to the church in Rome, "How then will they call on him in whom they have not believed? And how are they to believe in him of whom they have never heard? And how are they to hear without someone preaching? And how are they to preach unless they are sent? As it is written, "How beautiful are the feet of those who preach the good news!" (Rom. 10:14–15). The feet that run to carry our hands and faces that display the gospel must also bring along mouths ready to declare the gospel.

When we live Jesus[-]like lives but don't share the reason we can and do, we rob Jesus of his glory. He deserves the credit for what we do, not us. I understand that we often experience fear or insecurity when opportunities like these come up. I know that it's not easy for many of us to share Jesus with others.

I believe there are many reasons for this. First, as I said in Week 3, we are in a spiritual battle, so the enemy of our souls tries everything possible to keep us from speaking about Jesus. He can intimidate us to remain silent lest we be mocked or accused. Second, many of us love what people think of us more than we love people. So, in our fear of rejection, we keep our mouths shut. I pray you will love people more than their opinion of you. Third, most Christians have never tried to share their gospel hope, and therefore have never experienced the Spirit of God giving them words and boldness. When you do step out in faith, it's amaz-

ing how he gives you what you need. Fourth, many Christians just don't know the gospel very well or, if they do, don't practice sharing it with other believers very often. They aren't gospel fluent.

I pray that this book has given you a better knowledge of the gospel and some tools for how to grow in your gospel fluency. But the fifth reason for our silence is possibly the most concerning. I have found that most Christians don't really believe that their neighbors, friends, and family members will spend eternity apart from God if they don't have faith in Jesus. Judgment is coming. Hell is real. And apart from faith in Jesus Christ, people will miss out on enjoying life with God forever. It is so important that people are given the good news of Jesus. It's not our job to get them to believe it. That's the Spirit's job. We are called to live lives that demand gospel explanations and, when we have the opportunities, to give people Jesus as the answer for our hope. We might show how Jesus is better than what they have been trusting in. Maybe we listen to their stories and help them find hope, healing, and redemption by filling in the gaps with the true story. Or perhaps, just by listening, we discover their deeper longings and show how Jesus can do for them what nothing and no one else can. I can pray, display, and declare, but I can't save. That's God's job. So I will keep on listening, loving, blessing, sharing, and praying.

Thoughtfully read the following passages of Scripture related to today's theme. Take a few moments to write down words and phrases that particularly struck you, as well as any thoughts or personal applications they prompted. Make these words a prayer to God.

Luke 12:8-12

Romans 3:21-26

Romans 10:5-15

Declare the Gospel

WEEK 8, REFLECTION 1

To apply the concepts of this week's "Reading #1" in your everyday life, pray that God will open your eyes and guide you, then answer the following questions and complete the exercises.

1. Considering the content you read, in your own words describe the necessity of declaring the gospel, even in the midst of a life that displays what God is like.

2. Over the course of this *Handbook*, you've considered several ways Jesus has changed you. Spend a few moments worshiping God by looking back on weeks 1–7 and reflecting on specific areas of sin, unbelief, poor/unwise habits, etc. that God has changed. Write a few down, and simply declare—with your mouth or your pen—praise to God for his work in you.

3. In chapter 14 of *Gospel Fluency*, Jeff lists common reasons we hesitate to declare the gospel:

- First, we are in a spiritual battle, so the enemy of our souls tries everything possible to keep us from speaking about Jesus.

- Second, many of us love what people think of us more than we love people. So, in our fear of rejection, we keep our mouths shut.

- Third, most Christians have never tried to share their gospel hope, and therefore have never experienced the Spirit of God giving them words and boldness.

- Fourth, many Christians just don't know the gospel very well or, if they do, don't practice sharing it with other believers very often.

- But the fifth reason for our silence is possibly the most concerning. I have found that most Christians don't really believe that their neighbors, friends, and family members will spend eternity apart from God if they don't have faith in Jesus. Judgment is coming. Hell is real. And apart from faith in Jesus Christ, people will miss out on enjoying life with God forever.

Looking back over those words, circle all the reasons you feel you've been personally hindered at some point from sharing the gospel. In the space below, write any other things you feel have hindered you.

4. The Apostle Peter encourages followers of Jesus, "always be prepared to make a defense to anyone who asks you for a reason for the hope that is in you; yet do it with gentleness and respect..." (1 Peter 3:15). Sometimes we don't know how to share the gospel because we haven't thought about it enough to prepare ourselves to speak it when asked. If someone were to ask you about "the hope that is in you," how would you explain the good news of Jesus, in your own words? In other words, write down your understanding of the gospel, in light of your own hope.

5. Don't forget, last week's group exercise charged you to share the gospel with someone this week who doesn't know Jesus. As you consider various ways to declare the gospel to others and plan to share with someone, read—and pray that God will help you believe and rest in—this truth, from the letter to the Romans: "How then will they call on him in whom they have not believed? And how are they to believe in him of whom they have never heard? And how are they to hear without someone preaching? And how are they to preach unless they are sent? As it is written, 'How beautiful are the feet of those who preach the good news!'" (Rom 10:14-15). Consider writing out your thoughts and prayers as you reflect.

Grow in Love & Wisdom

WEEK 8, READING 2

Thoughtfully read the following excerpts, or for more context and a deeper dive, read the first part of chapter 15 of *Gospel Fluency*, stopping before the section titled "Wisdom for Manhood."

I hope that, through this book, you've gained more knowledge about the grace, mercy, and kindness of God through the good news of Jesus. I also pray you've become more fluent in speaking the gospel and listening with gospel ears. However, my greatest hope is that you love Jesus more now than when you started reading. Gospel fluency won't happen through you until it happens to you. You talk most about what you love most. I pray that I have helped you love Jesus more.

I also pray your love for people has grown. One of my concerns is that the tools and ideas in this book will become a hammer instead of a healing balm. The tendency of many well-intentioned people is to take a tool meant for love and instead hurt people with it by handling it without gentleness and care. We sometimes learn new truths and then think that if we just speak the truth to one another, that will be enough. But remember, Paul clarifies that we are called to speak the truth to one another in love (Eph. 4:15).

While instructing the church in Corinth on how to handle the truths he had given them, as well as the gifts God had given them, Paul says: "If I speak in the tongues of men and of angels, but have not love, I am a noisy gong or a clanging cymbal. And if I have prophetic powers, and understand all mysteries and all knowledge, and if I have all faith, so as to remove mountains, but have not love, I am nothing. If I give away all I have, and if I deliver up my body to be burned, but have not love, I gain nothing" (1 Cor. 13:1–3).

We can have right knowledge of the gospel, faith in the gospel, power to proclaim the gospel, and all the tools in the world to creatively do so, but still lack love. And if that is the case, our proclamation will mean nothing. At the heart of the gospel is the love of God. And if we speak about the love of God without love for people, the noise of our lives will drown out the words coming from our lips.

Do you love people? More specifically, do you love those who are different—who don't live like you or believe what you believe? If not, I want to encourage you to ask God to grant you his heart for people. Ask him to give you love for your neighbors, coworkers, family members, and friends. Invite him to fill your heart with his love and then ask him to enable you to feel what he feels for people.

Remember, he loved you while you were still a sinner—his enemy. Jesus suffered and died to forgive you of your sins, make you a child of God, and pour the love of God into your heart by his Spirit. So ask him to give you his heart for people. If you do, be ready. You will find that his love is greater than you imagined and deeper than you know.

The more I ask God to give me his heart for people, the more pain and passion I feel. I have more heart and heartbreak. I shed more tears and have more joy. I feel more sadness and exude more happiness. I observe more crying and I hear more laughter. I see depths of brokenness and watch miraculous healing. I have found that love is not all warm and fuzzy. It also hurts. But the more God's love flows into me, the more my love grows for him and others. As a result, the more careful, gentle, and wise I want to be. This is because love is embodied in wisdom—which is really where I want to end.

Wisdom isn't just increased knowledge, because knowledge without grace leads to pride, and pride precedes destruction in our lives and the lives of others. Wisdom is knowledge applied so that we do the right thing, at the right time, with the right motive, in the right way. Wisdom is gracious, loving, kind, and gentle.

When Peter charges the believers in Asia Minor to be prepared to give an answer for the hope that is in them—to give a gospel explanation for their godly lives—he says they should do it with gentleness and respect (1 Pet. 3:15). He then points to Jesus as the ultimate good news preacher (vv. 18–22). Likewise, Paul says to the church in Colossae: "Walk in wisdom toward outsiders, making the best use of the time. Let your speech always be gracious, seasoned with salt, so that you may know how you ought to answer each person" (Col. 4:5–6). Wisdom is timely. Wisdom is gracious. Wisdom is seasoned with salt, because it is healing, life-preserving, and taste-enhancing. It makes life better, not worse; fuller, not lesser; and more savory, not more sour.

When I was very young in my faith, I read James 1:5: "If any of you lacks wisdom, let him ask God, who gives generously to all without reproach, and it will be given him." I knew I lacked wisdom, so I started asking God for wisdom almost every day, sometimes several times a day. Since he had promised to give it to those who know they lack it and ask for it, I did. Since then, I have found that friends, both Christian and non-Christian, seek me out for counsel. As a result, I get to share the gospel more often. Thus, I don't just have wisdom from God to share, I also see the fruit of wisdom in my life.

Thoughtfully read the following passages of Scripture related to today's theme. Take a few moments to write down words and phrases that particularly struck you, as well as any thoughts or personal applications they prompted. Make these words a prayer to God.

1 Corinthians 13:1-3

Colossians 4:2-6

1 Peter 3:15-22

James 3:13-18

Grow in Love & Wisdom

WEEK 8, REFLECTION 2

To apply the concepts of this week's "Reading #2" in your everyday life, pray that God will open your eyes and guide you, then answer the following questions and complete the exercises.

1. Considering the content you read, in your own words define "love" and "wisdom," and describe why both are necessary in our declaration of the gospel.

2. How did God display love toward you, as he—through whatever or whomever he used—declared the good news of Jesus to you? How did he display his wisdom, in the specific way in which he saved you?

3. Every week's group discussion has reminded us of Ephesians 4:15, which encourages us to "speak the truth in love." We can have right knowledge of the gospel, faith in the gospel, power to proclaim the gospel, and all the tools in the world to creatively do so, but still lack love. And if that is the case, our proclamation will mean nothing. At the heart of the gospel is the love of God. And if we speak about the love of God without love for people, the noise of our lives will drown out the words coming from our lips. Think back to your non-believing friends from last week's Reflections. Considering your relationship with each, the lesser stories they live, and their areas of unbelief, in the columns below write ways that would be unloving, then loving, if you were to share the gospel with them. Maybe it's certain words; maybe it's situations or places; maybe it's the activity happening while you'd share. Whatever it is, how would they feel unloved, then loved, as you shared the gospel?

FRIEND	UNLOVING WAYS	LOVING WAYS

4. Biblical wisdom can be defined as "knowledge applied so that we do the right thing, at the right time, with the right motive, in the right way. Wisdom is gracious, loving, kind, and gentle." Spend some time praying that God would reveal areas of your life that don't reflect this (they might be defined by "unwise" or "foolishness"). In what specific areas, relationships, or ways doesn't your life reflect biblical wisdom? Write down at least three ways, then pray for wisdom. Feel free to invite others from your close community into your prayers.

5. As you consider your own need for love and wisdom, read—and pray that God will help you believe and rest in—this truth, from Paul's first letter to the Corinthians: "If I speak in the tongues of men and of angels, but have not love, I am a noisy gong or a clanging cymbal. And if I have prophetic powers, and understand all mysteries and all knowledge, and if I have all faith, so as to remove mountains, but have not love, I am nothing. If I give away all I have, and if I deliver up my body to be burned, but have not love, I gain nothing!" (1 Cor. 13:1-3). Consider writing out your thoughts and prayers as you reflect.

Conclusion

WEEK 8, READING 3

Thoughtfully read the following excerpts, or for more context and a deeper dive, read the second part of chapter 15 of *Gospel Fluency* as well as the "Conclusion." Begin with the section of chapter 15 titled "Wisdom for Manhood."

The apostle Paul says that Jesus is the wisdom of God (1 Cor. 1:24, 30). He is the true and better wisdom. He is also the means by which we get wisdom. The book of Proverbs advises us that the wisest thing we can do is get wisdom (Prov. 4:5, 7). It also instructs us that in order to . . . [give] wisdom, we need to get wisdom. In other words, we need to obtain wisdom to understand and apply wisdom. We can't make sense out of wisdom without the wisdom to do so.

How do we do this? How do we get wisdom to apply wisdom so we can show and tell the good news of Jesus graciously, lovingly, and gently?

We have to get Jesus. If you want the wisdom of God but haven't yet received God's wisdom for you in Jesus Christ, I invite you to surrender to him now. Receive what he has done for you in his life, death, and resurrection. Ask him to forgive you of your sins, cleanse you and make you clean, and come and dwell in you by his Spirit.

Maybe you believe you've already done that. Fine. However, don't neglect to ask God to keep giving you wisdom. You don't have enough yet. None of us does. We all need more wisdom from God to work through the situations, struggles, and opportunities that we face every day.

As James says, "If any of you lacks wisdom, let him ask God, who gives generously to all without reproach, and it will be given him." Ask God for wisdom and he will give you Jesus. And if you get Jesus, you will get everything you need for every part of your life. He is good news for the everyday stuff of life.

Don't put your confidence in your knowledge or skills. Don't just look to the principles or practices of this book—or any other book—to make you more effective. What you need, what I need, what we all need is Jesus. That's where wisdom begins. That's where wisdom ends.

That's the heart of this book. If you get Jesus, you get wisdom. Get wisdom from Jesus and you get everything else as well. He is better than everything else, and if you have him, then you'll give him.

Thoughtfully read the following passages of Scripture related to today's theme. Take a few moments to write down words and phrases that particularly struck you, as well as any thoughts or personal applications they prompted. Make these words a prayer to God.

Proverbs 4:5-9

John 1:1-18

1 Corinthians 1:20-31

Conclusion

WEEK 8, REFLECTION 3

To apply the concepts of this week's "Reading #3" in your everyday life, pray that God will open your eyes and guide you, then answer the following questions and complete the exercises.

1. Considering the content you read, in your own words describe how Jesus is the very wisdom of God himself.

2. What are other things you've looked to for wisdom? Write at least three other sources you've pursued in the first column below. In the second column, write some of the fruit—both good and not—each has produced. In the final column, describe how Jesus is a greater source of wisdom.

SOURCE OF WISDOM I'VE PURSUED	FRUIT OF PURSUING THAT SOURCE	JESUS' WISDOM COMPARED

3. What skills, knowledge, or abilities have you relied on instead of God to live a meaningful, productive life? Write at least three other sources you've pursued in the first column below. In the second column, write some of the fruit—both good and not—each has produced. In the final column, describe how Jesus is a greater source of wisdom.

SKILL, KNOWLEDGE, OR ABILITY THAT I'VE RELIED ON	FRUIT OF PURSUING THAT SOURCE	JESUS' WISDOM COMPARED

4. In what ways have the principles, practices, readings, reflections, discussions, and exercises of this *Handbook* helped train you in knowledge and skill, but also wisdom and love, in speaking the gospel to yourself, your community, and to others?

5. As you wrap up your final Reflection of this Handbook, read—and pray that God will help you believe and rest in—this truth: "Don't put your confidence in your knowledge or skills. Don't just look to the principles or practices of this book—or any other book—to make you more effective. What you need, what I need, what we all need is Jesus. That's where wisdom begins. That's where wisdom ends. That's the heart of this book. If you get Jesus, you get wisdom. Get wisdom from Jesus and you get everything else as well. He is better than everything else, and if you have him, then you'll give him." Write out your thoughts as you consider these ideas and turn them into prayers as you reflect.

Look Back

After completing your Readings and Reflections, and before your group meets this week, take a few moments to look over your readings and reflections: What have you learned? How has God shaped and impacted you? What do you especially want to remember, do, and/or share with your group this week?

Group Discussion

Looking back over this week's personal readings and reflection, discuss at least one or two of the following questions with a close community of friends. As you discuss, remember your commitment to be honest and to help each other "grow up in Christ" by "speaking truth in love" with each other.

1. What concepts were new, or especially stood out, from this week's readings? What was difficult from the readings? What questions do you have from the readings?

2. As a group, how would we together define "love" and "wisdom," and describe our need for each, in thoughtfully declaring the good news of Jesus, especially to those who don't know him?

Last week was about listening, learning, and displaying; this week is about acting, sharing, and declaring. As we talk about these areas more, let's remember that we rely on God the Spirit to give us the right words for any non-believing friends, and that he does so in his timing. And as we said last week, we must remember and celebrate that it's only God who can produce any fruit in our displays of the gospel.

3. What ways did we circle/write, in which we feel we've been hindered from declaring the gospel? How can we encourage and help each other overcome those barriers?

4. As we consider love and wisdom, let's celebrate God's goodness and encourage each other by sharing **a)** some of the ways he has displayed his love to you through others in the group, and/or **b)** ways you see his wisdom at work through your interactions with others.

5. Before you consider how to wrap up your group's past eight weeks together, share your answer to this question, from Reflection #3: In what ways have the principles, practices, readings, reflections, discussions, and exercises of this Handbook helped train you in knowledge and skill, but also wisdom and love, in speaking the gospel to yourself, your community, and to others?

6. Especially related to helping each other carry out God's mission of making disciples, are there any commitments your group needs to make to each other as you pursue "regularly rehearsing the gospel" in each other's lives together?

Group Exercise

This final exercise involves three parts: the first focuses on others; the other two focus on you. If your group is larger than about six people, you may want to divide into groups of three or four, to make sure everyone gets a chance to participate. This may be the most personal exercise to date, as you invite others to point out things in you that you may not see: be real, honest, prayerful, and loving, as you make these truths personal together.

First, have each person…

O Share things that God has revealed, in his wisdom and love, about the people you've felt called to share the gospel with. Specifically, what do they need to hear about the gospel? How do they need to see the work of the gospel in your life?

O Share the way you'd explain the good news of Jesus if asked on the spot. Share what you answered in Reflection #1, as our defenses of the hope within each of us.

Next, based on last week's assignment, think back to the way you shared the gospel this week.

O What words did you use? How wise and loving do you think you were?

O Did anything surprise you in your thoughts, words, or in the other person's response?

O How wise and loving did you feel the interaction was (both for you and the other person)?

O Any other thoughts or questions about your experience sharing the gospel?

After each person shares:

- Have the rest of the group pray for wisdom and love, in each person's desire and attempts to share the gospel with those specific people, and for the people with whom the gospel was shared by each person in your group.

- Listen for elements of the story of God in each person's explanation of the gospel: How do they mention identity, sin, salvation, and hope? Who's the hero of the story? How is the gospel clearly good news? Spend some time encouraging each other in your gospel declaration.

✳ NOTE ✳

Enrich your learning and experience for this week by watching the companion video at **saturatetheworld.com/gf**

NEXT STEPS

This is your group's final meeting with this *Gospel Fluency Handbook*. On the next page, we close this resource with a word of encouragement. After your group prays for each other, look over the next page's "Conclusion" together, and make plans for what will happen with your group now that you've come to the end of this journey.

Here are some ideas you may want to consider as you discuss next steps:

If your group was only meeting for this study, decide whether or not you want to disband (or if some people want to stay together while others go).

- If you're disbanding, how can you make sure that everyone lands in meaningful community or begins leading a community of their own?

- If you're staying together, what might be the content for future weeks? Another study, and if so, which one? Some specific time to practice the things you've learned together in this *Handbook*? Time for prayer, recreation, or serving together? Etc.

One reason that Old Testament Israel continued to walk away from hoping in God's promised Messiah was because they forgot what God had taught them. Consider meeting once more with no agenda except to remember and process what God has done in you, individually and together, over these past weeks.

- What have you learned?

- What has God changed in you?

- Since God consistently draws people deeper, has your definition of the gospel, or the way you'd tell your story with Jesus as the hero, changed over the past weeks?

- How have you seen that applied, personally, with other followers of Jesus or in your mission field?

- What's still hard and how can you help each other?

- What are you hoping God might continue to do as you grow in gospel fluency?

If you want to go deeper into related content, the *Saturate Field Guide* is a similar resource we have produced to help apply gospel fluency to following Jesus in the everyday stuff of life. Starting with Jesus and discipleship in general, it walks through identities and rhythms by which we can display and declare the gospel, especially in the context of missional communities.

Many other resources are available for you and your community at saturatetheworld.com

Conclusion

We know that reading a book—or rehearsing stories, or even completing the reflections, discussions, and group exercises you've done over these past weeks—are not in themselves sufficient to make you gospel fluent, any more than reading a book on Spanish grammar, memorizing Spanish vocabulary, and learning Spanish culture will make you fluent in Spanish. It's necessary, but not sufficient. It doesn't end here. You have to speak the gospel—a lot. You need to hear it. You must be immersed in it. And you need to love it. You need to love the gospel.

Don't put this *Handbook* down and just move on. Your training has just begun. Start regularly rehearsing the truths about Jesus over and over again in your mind. Invite the Spirit of God to wash over your heart with the depths of his love as we see it in the truth of the gospel. Regularly take captive your thoughts to bring them into submission to what is true of Jesus and what is true of you if your life is in Jesus. Surround yourself with people who love Jesus and want to grow in speaking the truths of Jesus into the everyday stuff of life. Be with them a lot. And make sure you invite them to speak into your life and into your heart. Submit yourself to others who want to give you Jesus, not just another self-help technique. And make sure you give them Jesus as well. He is the hope of the world! He is the changer of hearts! He is the only name under heaven given to us by which we might be saved.

And as you speak Jesus to one another, do it with grace, wisdom, and love, all of which you can get from him in limitless supply. As you receive it from him, give him credit for what he gives and what he does. Keep speaking Jesus because you talk about what works—and Jesus works; the gospel works. Keep growing in your love for Jesus, because you talk most about what you love most. The gospel is the love of God that works because it is the power of God for salvation for all who believe. So don't be ashamed! Tell yourself. Tell your friends. Tell your family members. Tell everyone that you have some good news for them—good news that will change them forever.

God loves them. Jesus lived, died, and rose again for them. Their lives—every single part—can be changed forever as a result. It's true for you as well. Don't forget it. There really isn't anything better to talk about than Jesus. There also isn't anything better for meeting our every need than Jesus.

So let's start learning together how to speak Jesus into the everyday stuff of life together, every day and everywhere. *Gospel fluency class is now in session.*

Appendix

Defining Theological Concepts

DEFINING THEOLOGICAL CONCEPTS

All definitions are our own unless marked with an asterisk (*). Asterisked definitions are from Wayne Grudem, *Systematic Theology* (Zondervan, 1994); we find Dr. Grudem's definitions to be both comprehensive and understandable, which is a unique blend when it comes to deep theological terms! Clarifications in parentheses are added.

Ascension*
The rising of Jesus from the earth into heaven forty days after his resurrection

Atonement*
The work Christ did in his life and death to earn our salvation

Baptism
Especially in reference to Jesus, an act of obedience in which Jesus modeled submission to God, and foreshadowed death (by entering the water) and new life (by rising out of it), an act followed by many Christians throughout history upon repentance of sin and proclaiming trust in Jesus; the moment at which Jesus' ministry was inaugurated by God the Father through a voice from heaven, and confirmed by the dove-like appearance of God the Spirit, who descended on Jesus upon coming out of the water.

Forgiveness

The primary accomplishment promised in the gospel message; the putting away of our sin in God's eyes, based on the finished work of Christ, with the assurance in God's promise to restore all those who repent to an eternal life with God

The Gospel

The power of God for salvation for all who believe.

Gospel Fluency

The growing ability to speaking the truths of Jesus into the everyday stuff of life, so that all parts of our lives grow up into Christ and are eventually fully transformed by and submitted to Jesus Christ.

Gospel Fluent Community

A group of people who are **1)** growing in faith in the gospel as evidenced by people confessing their sins to one another regularly, **2)** growing in confidence that Jesus fully atoned for their sins, and **3)** extending grace and forgiveness to one another.

Grace through faith

Grace* is "God's goodness toward those who deserve only punishment" (for sin); faith* is "trust or dependence on God based on the fact that we take him at his word and believe what he has said." The Apostle Paul, most overtly in Ephesians 2, writes that it is by faith that the promise of God's grace is made real in the lives of people; God gives us faith to believe in God's grace—this leads to both "saving faith: trust in Jesus Christ as a living person of forgiveness of sins and for eternal life with God," as well as grace for "sanctification: [the] progressive work of God and man that makes us more and more free from sin and more like Jesus in our actual lives." (One aspect of grace through faith is the ability to believe God, his word, and his promises, to the point that his truth overcomes any disbelief in our lives. This leads to greater trust, obedience, and submission to God as Savior and Lord of every aspect of life.)

Humility
The mindset and actions of putting others first, especially poignant if one has the right to a higher position (Jesus displayed the utmost humility, as the Lord of the Universe became a servant to mankind, even to the point of death on their behalf)

Kingship*
One of the three offices fulfilled by Christ in which he rules over the church and the universe (the other two being Prophet and Priest)

Obedience
Especially in reference to Jesus, the reality that by the power of God the Spirit, God the Son (Jesus) was the only human on earth to live in perfect obedience—in will and works; in thought, motivation, and deed—to the will, commands, and purposes of God the Father.

Propitiation*
A sacrifice that bears God's wrath to the end and in doing so changes God's wrath toward us into favor

Resurrection*
A rising from the dead into a new kind of life not subject to sickness, aging, deterioration, or death

Sending of God the Spirit
In reference to Jesus, the promise toward the end of his earthly ministry that he would send a "helper" to his followers, by whom they would receive power to carry forth his words and works, and fulfill the ministry that Jesus began on earth (the accomplishment of this was first seen at Pentecost in Acts 2, and is true for every believer upon repenting of sin, and trusting and following Jesus as their Savior and Lord)

Sinlessness*
The state of being totally free from sin (Christian orthodoxy holds that Jesus, and among humans only Jesus, lived a perfectly sinless life.)

Spirit-ledness
The motive and mindset of pursuing and following God the Father's will, by submission to God the Spirit's work in one's life; often accompanied by fruit, giftedness, and varying displays of power, action, or speech for accomplishing God's work (among humans, only Jesus was fully Spirit-led)

Substitution
Jesus' act of taking the place of mankind as a sacrifice to receive all of God's wrath and judgment for sin, toward those who believe in and follow him as their Savior and Lord

What's Next?

A few recommendations after the *Gospel Fluency Handbook*...

Want to effectively live out of your gospel indentity?	Want to grow as a disciple with 2-3 others?	Want to disciple kids in the truths of Jesus?
Check out **Saturate Field Guide**	Check out **Growing in Christ Together**	Check out **Gospel Basics for Kids**

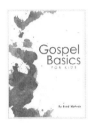

www.saturatetheworld.com

facebook.com/ **SaturateTheWorld**

twitter.com/ **SaturateWorld**

instagram.com/ **SaturateTheWorld**

Are you a LEADER?

Do you want to see your church family transition from Sunday to everyday? Do you want to see your small groups transform into healthy, on-mission disciple-makers?

Don't go it alone. Saturate can help.

COMMUNITY	COACHING	RESOURCES	TRAINING	CONSULTATIONS
Shared learning with experts and fellow disciple-makers	Process to help you implement a disciple-making culture	Video, digital, and print materials to help you lead	Events to equip you in everyday disciple-making	Personal and customized training from our staff